e-policy

CONQWEST, INC.

84 October Hill Rd, Bldg 7, Holliston, MA 01746 USA
1-888-234-7404   508-893-0111   Fax: 508-893-0110

e-policy

*How to Develop Computer,
E-mail, and Internet Guidelines
to Protect Your Company
and Its Assets*

Michael R. Overly

AMACOM
AMERICAN MANAGEMENT ASSOCIATION
New York • Atlanta • Boston • Chicago • Kansas City • San Francisco • Washington, D.C.
Brussels • Mexico City • Tokyo • Toronto

This book is available at a special discount when ordered in bulk quantities. For information, contact Special Sales Department, AMACOM, a division of American Management Association, 1601 Broadway, New York, NY 10019.

This publication is designed to provide accurate and authoritative information in regard to the subject matter covered. It is sold with the understanding that the publisher is not engaged in rendering legal, accounting, or other professional service. If legal advice or other expert assistance is required, the services of a competent professional person should be sought.

Library of Congress Cataloging-in-Publication Data

Overly, Michael R.
    E-policy: how to develop computer, E-mail, and Internet
  guidelines to protect your company and its assets / Michael R.
  Overly.
        p.   cm.
      Includes index.
      ISBN 0-8144-7996-0
      1. Business enterprises—Computer networks—Security measures.
    2. Computer security.   3. Electronic mail systems—Security
    measures.   I. Title.
    HD30.38.O94   1999
    658.4'78—dc21   98-26077
                                                        CIP

© 1999 SciTech Publishing, Inc.
All rights reserved.
Printed in the United States of America.

Printing number
10 9 8 7 6 5

The law in this area changes rapidly and is subject to differing interpretations. It is up to the reader to review the current state of the law with a qualified attorney before relying on it. Neither the author or the publisher of this book makes any guarantees or warranties regarding the outcome of the uses to which the material is put. This book is sold with the understanding that the author and publisher are not engaged in rendering legal or professional service. If legal advice or other professional assistance is required, the services of a competent person should be sought. Purchasing this book does not create an attorney-client relationship.

Contents

Foreword

"One of the greatest distinctions, and dangers, of e-mail is that it is treated far more informally than other forms of business communications. People often use it to express thoughts, emotions, and opinions that they would never memorialize in a traditional written document." – Michael Overly

E-mail has become a blessing and a curse to professionals the world over. On one hand, the Internet has enabled high-speed, affordable global communications that are transforming the way companies do business. On the other hand, it has introduced a myriad of threats ranging from network downtime to legal action. A virus hidden in an e-mail attachment shuts down your network; confidential information leaks via e-mail; offensive material in an e-mail sparks a discrimination lawsuit—all of these are probable scenarios, and as you will read in this book, may companies have had the dubious honor of firsthand experience with at least one of them.

There are a number of ways companies and individuals can protect themselves from the threats of online communication, but such defenses are usually deployed after the fact—after costly network repairs or a multi-million dollar lawsuit. Underestimating the power of e-mail to wreak havoc on your organization can be a costly mistake, and this book is an excellent tool for preventing just that.

Overly tackles this issue head-on, providing insight and solutions for how companies can use sound policymaking to avoid the legal repercussions of Internet communication. Some of the topics covered in this book include the privacy rights of employees, discrimination and harassment issues, copyright infringement and spamming. With pithy commentary on the most recent legislation surrounding Internet communication, example policies and the "six essentials for every good policy," Overly's book is an invaluable resource for every organization that uses e-mail.

As the use of e-mail grows, so will the risks of using it. *e-policy: How to Develop Computer, E-mail, and Internet Guidelines to Protect Your Company and Its Assets* provides a starting point for protecting your organization from the legal threats of e-mail, and is an excellent reference no executive bookshelf should be without.

Peter Kershaw
Content Technologies

Part I

GETTING YOUR
FEET WET

Introduction

Almost every aspect of business now revolves around the computer. Moreover, the very role of computers in business is changing from being merely an efficient repository and processor of information to an effective means of global communication. These advances have not come without a cost. Employee use of a business's computer resources, including e-mail and Internet access, can subject a company to potential legal liability, compromise confidential information, and result in unnecessary increases in computing costs. Examples of these problems abound:

- Businesses have spent many millions of dollars litigating and settling lawsuits arising out of employee abuse and misuse of e-mail. Employees use e-mail to circulate inappropriate jokes, harass and discriminate against coworkers, and defame other businesses.
- Trade secrets and other highly sensitive business information stored on computers have been stolen or inadvertently compromised by employees.
- Employee use of the Internet for nonbusiness-related activities has seriously compromised corporate security and resulted in countless millions of dollars in lost productivity and increased computing costs.
- Searches of business networks routinely turn up hundreds of megabytes of pornographic material and illegal software loaded by employees.

To reduce, and possibly eliminate, some of these negative factors, businesses can take three steps:

1. Adopt written policies on computer and e-mail use that specifically define the rights and obligations of employees regarding computer resources.
2. Conduct training and awareness seminars for employees regarding proper use of their computers and Internet and e-mail access.
3. Install appropriate monitoring and filtering software to prevent access to inappropriate material and to identify problem employees.

Although each of these steps is addressed in this book, the primary focus is on developing written computer and e-mail policies for business. Developing and implementing such a policy can be a complicated process, involving substantive issues of law, employee relations, and security. This book provides a thorough introduction to each of these topics. In addition, a wide range of complete policies, guidelines, and other useful documents are included in the example policies of Appendix A. To further assist the reader in preparing a draft policy, sample clauses are included throughout the text. The goal is to provide the reader with a one-stop resource for preparing a range of computer and e-mail use policies.

The Need for Written Policies

Despite the growing use of computers and Internet and e-mail access in the workplace and its the concomitant potential for liability, only about one-fourth of all businesses have established written guidelines relating to employee use of these systems. Of those businesses that have adopted written guidelines, few adequately address the myriad problems that can arise. Businesses must be aware of the potential pitfalls that go along with this new technology and protect against them by adopting appropriate guidelines and policies.

In the event of a lawsuit, having a well-written policy may mean the difference between liability for damages and early dismissal of the action. An example illustrates the advantage of having a formal e-mail policy.

A system manager at Nissan Motor accidentally discovered a sexually explicit e-mail message while conducting a training seminar for new employees. The incident was reported to a supervisor, who ordered a review of the sending employee's e-mail, as well as the e-mail of fellow workgroup members.

Despite several warnings, the employees continued sending inappropriate e-mail, resulting in their termination. The employees sued Nissan, arguing among other things that the company had violated their right of privacy in reviewing their e-mail.[1] Nissan was able to prevail early in the lawsuit because it had an explicit e-mail policy, which prevented the employees from arguing they had a right of privacy in their messages. Without such a policy, Nissan would likely have incurred significantly higher litigation costs and risked liability for substantial damages.

Businesses that have failed to adopt and enforce appropriate policies have not fared as well as Nissan in litigation. For example, a school employee's reprimand for sending e-mail that ridiculed the school's curriculum was found to be unwarranted because the school had no rules or regulations in place governing the use of its computer and e-mail system.[2]

This book is organized around accomplishing the three goals of every effective computer and e-mail policy:

1. Reducing, and if possible eliminating, potential legal liability to employees and third parties (discussed in Parts II and III of this book)
2. Protecting confidential, proprietary information of the business from theft or unauthorized disclosure to third parties (Part IV)
3. Preventing waste of business computer resources (Part IV)

Endnotes

1. *Bourke v. Nissan Motor Co.*, (CA Super. Ct., 1991, docket no. YC 003979).
2. *In re Conneaut School District and Conneaut Education Association,* 104 Lab. Arb. (BNA) 909 (1995).

Chapter 1

E-mail: The Prime Mover

Many of the problems, and most of the lawsuits, that result from employee use of computers in the workplace revolve around electronic mail (e-mail). Because of its importance, much of the discussion in this book relates to problems arising from use of e-mail. This chapter provides an overview of this important medium of communication.

E-mail is revolutionizing the way many businesses communicate with their employees, vendors, and customers. Because it is economical, fast, and easy to use, for thousands of businesses and tens of millions of individuals throughout the world e-mail is quickly becoming the preferred method of communicating.

Corporate networks, or intranets, have seen e-mail evolve from purely a method whereby technical personnel can exchange ideas to an essential means for disseminating information to employees, promoting intracompany communications, and tracking employee productivity and work quality.

The volume of e-mail, particularly over the Internet, is staggering. More than 1 million messages pass through the Internet every hour. An estimated 2.7 trillion e-mail messages were sent in 1997. Nearly 7 trillion messages annually are projected by the year 2000. Even within a single organization, the volume of e-mail can be substantial. One large American company estimates that its employees send more than a million messages across company networks every day.[1]

E-mail has quietly become the "killer" application on the Internet. Although many businesses may not be able to spend thousands or tens of thousands of dollars developing and maintaining a site on the World Wide Web (the Web), even the smallest business can afford e-mail. In fact, if a business is willing to tolerate a few advertisements, several commercial online services provide employees with e-mail accounts at no charge.

The Advantages of E-mail

E-mail can provide employees with an efficient and economical means of communicating among themselves and with customers and vendors even when the intended recipient is in a remote office, working at home, or traveling.

Wide Use

According to most estimates, between 70 and 80 percent of businesses in the United States have access to e-mail. When you add to that several million home users, you have a method of communication that is both widespread and here to stay. Businesses that neglect this new medium or are slow to exploit it will quickly find themselves at a disadvantage in the marketplace. Today, a growing number of businesses and consumers expect that you will be able to communicate with them using this new medium.

Speed of Delivery

One of e-mail's strongest features is its speed of delivery. E-mail messages generally arrive at their destinations within minutes, or at the most a couple of hours, of transmission. With the possible exception of a fax, delivery time for e-mail is almost always faster than any other form of business communication. Even if it did not enjoy the clear advantage of speed, e-mail would still have a number of unique features that go far beyond what a fax can offer, as the following sections affirm.

Economics

Apart from face-to-face encounters, e-mail is one of the most cost-effective methods of communication ever invented. In general, the cost of Internet access does not vary with the volume of e-mail sent. This means the cost is the same whether a business sends ten e-mails a day or a thousand an hour. Moreover, there is no postage online. The cost of sending a 2-page e-mail across town is the same as sending an 800-page message to Japan.

Attachments

The ability to include attachments with e-mail is one of its most important features. Attachments allow documents to be sent "in format" along with the e-mail. For example, a business uses Excel® to create a spreadsheet that it wants to send to its accountant for revision. The business can send the accountant an e-mail with the spreadsheet as an attachment. On receipt, the accountant uses his copy of Excel to edit the spreadsheet directly. Try that with a fax.

Accessibility

E-mail provides the means for today's mobile employees to send and receive messages and attachments while away from the office. Because e-mail is routed over commercial computer networks such as the Internet, employees can send and receive messages from any location where they have access to a computer and a telephone. This means that employees can communicate whenever and wherever they want. Instead of being tied to a particular telephone number or physical address, e-mail provides employees with a "virtual" address that can be accessed, usually with a local call, almost anywhere in the world.

Ease of Forwarding

Ease of forwarding is another advantage of e-mail. Because e-mail is stored digitally, it can be forwarded any number of times with no degradation of quality. With a fax, you are lucky to be able to read the original, let alone one that has been faxed several times from one recipient to another. In most instances, if you want to forward a fax to someone, you generally have to send a hard copy to them by messenger or overnight delivery.

Forwarding e-mail is also far easier than using a fax. As with all e-mail, forwarding a message takes only a couple of key strokes. This makes communicating easy and economical (because there is no incremental cost in forwarding a message). The ability to quickly and easily share a message even with an attachment also makes collaboration with multiple parties straightforward.

However, ease of forwarding is also a substantial disadvantage of e-mail. We now look at the drawbacks of the medium.

The Disadvantages of E-mail

Communication at a Cost

The growing use of e-mail in business has not come without costs. As online communications have become ever more ubiquitous, so has their role and importance in legal disputes. E-mail has already been the focus of dozens of lawsuits involving claims of sexual harassment, discrimination, breach of contract, fraud, defamation, and theft of trade secrets. Employee use of e-mail also raises concerns about security of sensitive business information and potential waste of corporate computer resources. This section outlines some of the inherent problems and concerns resulting from use of e-mail in the workplace.

Electronic "Postcards"

At present, e-mail is transmitted across the Internet using the Simple Mail Transfer Protocol (SMTP).[2] This protocol has virtually no security or privacy features built into it. In particular, messages are not encrypted or encoded in any way. Consequently, e-mail is like an electronic postcard; messages can be read by anyone who comes in contact with them. This is why many users have turned to commercially available encryption programs to shield their messages from prying eyes. If a message is not encoded with one of these programs, the sender should always assume that the message can and will be read by unintended parties.

Informal Treatment

One of the greatest distinctions, and dangers, of e-mail is that it is treated far more informally than other forms of business communications. People often use it to express thoughts, emotions, and opinions that they would never memorialize in a conventional written document. In large part, this may be because e-mail doesn't look like a normal letter or memorandum; ordinarily, there is no formal letterhead or signature line on e-mail.

Another reason e-mail is treated so informally is the problem of perceived impermanence. People wrongly believe that if they delete a piece of e-mail it is gone forever. In fact, using widely available software, deleted messages can be "undeleted" days, weeks, or even months after they were thought deleted.

Even if a message cannot be undeleted, backup copies of the e-mail may exist on the sender's or recipient's personal computer or on their employers' networks. If the e-mail was sent through a commercial service (e.g., Prodigy, America Online, or CompuServe) or the Internet, the e-mail may have passed through several computers before being delivered. Each computer in the chain between the sender and the recipient may, and normally does, retain a copy of the e-mail for archival purposes.

Thinking of e-mail as an informal, ephemeral means of communication has been the cause of many lawsuits and employment disputes. Employees who have circulated inappropriate jokes or cartoons or who have sent sexually explicit messages have found themselves and/or their employers defendants in lawsuits for discrimination, sexual harassment, and defamation, among other things.

Ease of Circulation and Copying

Although the ease with which e-mail may be copied and forwarded is a great advantage, it is also a significant drawback. When you send a message to someone, you have no control over whether that person keeps your message confidential or circulates it to any number of other people-or posts it on the Internet, where it may be viewed by thousands of people. This is a particular concern if your message contains sensitive or trade secret information, or if it is a communication with your attorney that may be protected by the attorney-client privilege. In these instances, disclosure to unintended parties may result in substantial harm to your business and potential waiver of the attorney-client privilege.

Sexual Harassment and Discrimination

Claims of sexual harassment and discrimination based on e-mail are particularly prevalent and have resulted in substantial settlements.

In one recent case, a woman filed a lawsuit against her former employer for age discrimination. Her suit appeared frivolous because her former employer had carefully handled her termination. The termination was referred to as "picture perfect by human resources standards." The company expected to quickly dispose of the litigation or, at most, settle for nuisance value.

But during the discovery phase of the lawsuit, the woman's attorney hired a computer consultant to examine the company's e-mail system. The consultant successfully recovered a previously deleted message from the company's president to the head of the personnel department. In the e-mail, the president used blatantly discriminatory language to order the woman's termination. Shortly after discovery of the message, the company settled the case for $250,000.

In another case, Chevron paid $2.2 million to settle a sexual harassment lawsuit brought by a large group of women who alleged, among other things, that a subsidiary of Chevron permitted its internal e-mail system to be used for transmitting sexually offensive messages. One such message listed "25 reasons beer is better than women."

Ease of Misaddressing

Because e-mail is typically addressed by selecting the recipient's name from an online directory, it is very easy to click on the wrong name and send the message to an unintended person. This is a particular problem when you are sending a message to multiple recipients, and it may not be obvious that you included an incorrect name in the "To:" field of the e-mail. Care should always be taken to ensure that e-mail is properly addressed.

Potential Seizure of Computer Systems

Improper use of e-mail can also lead to seizure of a business's entire computer system. If an employee or other individual who is authorized to use the system engages in illegal conduct (for example, sending fraudulent or threatening e-mail, conducting an illegal business), the government may seize the computer system to preserve evidence.

This is exactly what happened to a small computer game company that allowed its computer system to be used for the exchange of e-mail between game players and other interested individuals. During the course of an investigation concerning computer hackers, federal authorities discovered that one of the e-mail accounts on the company's computer contained stolen telephone company data. The Secret Service obtained a search warrant, raided the company, and seized its computer system, which seriously disrupted the company's business for months.[3]

The potential for seizure of a business's computer because of employee misuse of its e-mail system is a very real possibility. The U.S. Justice Department has issued Guidelines for Search and Seizure of Computer Systems, which provide that unless a business is prepared to cooperate with an investigation, seizure of computers is entirely appropriate and within the power of law enforcement investigators.

E-mail Forgery

Another hazard of e-mail is that it can generally be changed or altered without leaving a trace. A recent case involving Lawrence Ellison, the CEO of Oracle Corp., illustrates the elusive nature of electronic documents. A former employee named Adelyn Lee brought suit against Ellison and Oracle, alleging she had been wrongfully terminated because she refused to have sex with Ellison. As proof of her claim, Adelyn introduced an incriminating e-mail from her supervisor to Ellison that read, "I have terminated Adelyn per your request." It was later discovered the e-mail was a forgery. Cellular telephone records proved the supervisor was driving his car at the time the message was purportedly sent.

Creation of Jurisdiction

Employee misuse of e-mail may also subject employers to the jurisdiction of courts in other states—and even other countries—in which the employer has never even conducted business. Several courts have found that sending e-mail into their states is sufficient cause to exercise jurisdiction over the sender.[4] This means that if an employee uses a business's e-mail system to send messages into another state and a lawsuit arises from those messages, the business may be forced to defend itself in that jurisdiction.

"Spam" Attacks

There is a growing trend for disgruntled employees and customers to intentionally use e-mail to provoke a "spam attack" against targeted businesses. (In this context, spam is unsolicited "junk" e-mail.) Suppose someone is judged to have violated the etiquette of the Internet. The offender might find, among other things, that the e-mail account is swamped by protest messages, fax machines are clogged with thousands of pages of random text, and the switchboard is shut down by hundreds of telephone calls automatically placed by computers. The purpose of the attack, clearly, is to disrupt the offender's business.

Samsung Electronics America was recently the subject of just such a spam attack. A disgruntled customer sent a large number of "cease and desist" messages to apparently random individuals accusing them of hacking and other crimes. The customer doctored the messages to appear as though they were official e-mail sent by Samsung's attorney. The recipient's responses ranged from minor annoyance to threatened legal action. Samsung received 6,000-10,000 angry e-mail messages a day about the fake letter. The bogus messages may have permanently damaged Samsung's reputation.[5]

E-mail in the Larger Context of Business

Duty to Preserve E-mail in Pending Litigation

Businesses should also understand their duty to preserve e-mail that relates to a pending lawsuit. Destruction of e-mail, whether intentional or unintentional, may result in a claim of spoliation of evidence. In a recent wrongful-termination lawsuit, a jury found that a major aerospace company had intentionally destroyed relevant e-mail. The jury awarded the plaintiff $20,000 for intentional spoliation of evidence and $60,000 in punitive damages.[6]

Unintentional destruction of evidence is particularly likely in large corporations. By the time a message from the corporation's attorney winds its way down to the information systems department, old e-mail on backup tapes may already have been overwritten as part of the normal backup process. Businesses must be sensitive to their duty to preserve evidence and act quickly when a dispute arises.

Growing Focus of Discovery in Lawsuits

As e-mail becomes ever more ubiquitous, so will its use in litigation. Given the informality of most e-mail messages, attorneys have found them to be fertile ground for telling admissions, which can often be very damaging. More than one recent case has turned on the discovery of an electronic "smoking gun."

In one well-known case, Siemens Solar Industries purchased the solar energy subsidiary of Atlantic Richfield Co. (ARCO). Following the sale, Siemens discovered e-mail in ARCO's computer system showing that at the time of the transaction ARCO knew the solar technology was not commercially viable. "We will attempt to finesse past Siemens the fact that we have had a great amount of trouble in successfully transitioning the [new] technology from the lab to the manufacturing floor," wrote an ARCO employee. "As it appears [the technology] is a pipe dream, let Siemens have the pipe." Siemens sued ARCO, alleging ARCO misrepresented the ability of its subsidiary to develop the new technology.

This case and others like it have prompted many attorneys to focus their discovery efforts on e-mail and other electronic documents. Responding to a discovery request that includes e-mail can be an expensive and laborious task for most businesses. Backup tapes, individual workstations, laptops, home computers, and the company's network may all have to be searched to locate responsive e-mail. Such searches are often complicated by the fact that employees do not have set directories into which they store their e-mail, thus requiring a time-consuming search of the entire computer system.

Although most businesses have implemented retention policies for written documents that require destruction of the documents after a certain period of time, few have adopted similar procedures for e-mail. As a result, the volume of e-mail that must be reviewed to respond to a discovery demand may be enormous. Every business should consider adopting a policy that requires e-mail to be deleted after a specified period of time. On many systems, deletion of old e-mail can be accomplished automatically.

In addition to adopting a retention policy, businesses should take steps to ensure that their employees use e-mail appropriately and professionally. One step is to create a formal e-mail policy that specifically defines the obligations and duties of every e-mail user. In particular, the policy should make clear that employees are expected to use the same care and discretion in drafting e-mail as they would for any other written business communication. If employees exercise that degree of care in drafting their e-mail, many lawsuits for defamation, discrimination, and harassment can easily be avoided.

Potential Waste of Business Computer Resources

Employee waste of computer resources is a growing concern for business. Computer networks have finite bandwidth (the ability to transmit information) and limited storage capacity. Employee misuse and abuse of these resources may result in increased network traffic, slower response time for legitimate business activity, and increased costs for data storage. For example, junk e-mail sent to employees cost one multinational corporation approximately one dollar per employee per day— a considerable sum given its 55,000 employees.

Summary

E-mail is a unique medium, quite unlike traditional written communications. Businesses must be aware of the potential pitfalls that go along with this new form of communication and protect against them by adopting appropriate corporate policies for use of e-mail.

SAMPLE CLAUSES IN E-MAIL POLICY

Forwarding e-mail. Users[7] may not forward e-mail to any other person or entity without the express permission of the sender. [*E-mail frequently contains confidential, proprietary, or even trade secret information. What is meant for a single reader may not be meant for widespread distribution. Rather than rely on each employee's judgment as to whether a particular message may be forwarded, many companies are adopting a "bright-line" no-forwarding policy.*]

Chain e-mail. Users may not initiate or forward chain e-mail. Chain e-mail is a message sent to a number of people asking each recipient to send copies with the same request to a specified number of others.

[*Chain mail is growing ever more popular on corporate networks and is quickly becoming a substantial drain on computer resources. The circulation of a chain letter increases in geometrical progression as long as the instructions are followed by all recipients. This can seriously degrade network performance and consume substantial amounts of valuable disk space.*]

Communicating information. Content of all communications should be accurate. Users should use the same care in drafting e-mail and other electronic documents as they would for any other written communication. Anything created on the computer may, and likely will, be reviewed by others.

[*This clause reminds employees of their duty to be careful in authoring messages and of the fact that their messages may be reviewed by third persons.*]

E-mail retention. Unless directed to the contrary by your supervisor, employees should discard inactive e-mail after sixty (60) days.

[*Some businesses may be subject to federal and state laws and regulations governing mandatory retention of business records and electronic communication. These retention laws may require you to maintain files or documents for a specified period of time. Your business may also be under a duty to refrain from deleting files if they are relevant to a threatened or pending lawsuit. Destruction of the documents with knowledge of the lawsuit may lead to liability for spoliation of evidence. Consult with an attorney in each of these instances to determine your rights.*]

Endnotes

1. See Glassberg, "Electronic Communication: An Ounce of Policy is Worth a Pound of Cure," *Business Horizons* (July 1996), for discussion of Du Pont's use of e-mail.
2. SMTP is a server-to-server protocol; other protocols are used to access the messages. For more information on SMTP, see RFC 821, available at www.nsi.org. An "RFC" is an acronym for

"Request for Comments." RFCs are created and posted online to describe new or proposed features for the Internet. Network Solutions Inc. has collected most of the RFCs and made them available on their Web site.

3. *Steve Jackson Games Inc. v. U.S. Secret Service*, 36 F.3d 457 (5th Cir. 1994).

4. See, for example *Hall v. LaRonde*, 66 Cal. Rptr. 2d 399 (1997), wherein telephone calls and e-mail may be deemed sufficient to exercise jurisdiction of a resident of New York.

5. You can read about the scam on Samsung's Web site: www.samsung.com.

6. *Shaw v. Hughes Aircraft Co.* (Los Angeles Sup. Ct.); see also "Somebody Destroyed the Evidence," *Corporate Legal Times*, vol. 7, no. 70 (Sept. 1997).

7. To ensure that the policy applies to the widest range of computer users, which can include individuals who are not employees, the term *users* is frequently substituted for *employees*. *Users* refers to all employees, independent contractors, consultants, temporary workers, and other persons or entities who use or have access to a business's computer resources.

Part II
POTENTIAL CLAIMS BY EMPLOYEES

Chapter 2

Employee Privacy Rights

To Peek or Not to Peek, That Is the Question

To protect themselves from liability and to ensure that their computer resources are used only for authorized purposes, employers must have the right to monitor employee files and e-mail. In response to such monitoring, employees have claimed, among other things, invasion of their common-law right of privacy, violation of state privacy laws, violation of the Fourth Amendment's protections against unreasonable searches and seizures, and violation of the Electronic Communications Privacy Act of 1986. Because these claims may result in substantial liability to the employer, computer use policies should be tailored to minimize the likelihood of a successful claim.

Common-Law Invasion of Privacy

Almost every state recognizes a common-law[1] right of privacy. Violations of the right of privacy are punishable by a tort[2] action for damages. The common law tort of invasion of privacy is generally defined this way: "One who intentionally intrudes, physically or otherwise, upon the solitude or seclusion of another, or his personal affairs or concerns, is subject to liability to the other for invasion of privacy, if the intrusion would be highly offensive to a reasonable person."[3]

In other words, for an employee to successfully maintain a claim for invasion of privacy against an employer, the employee must prove that she had an expectation of privacy, and that the employer engaged in highly offensive monitoring (and in some states, that the employer published the information received from the monitoring).

Another privacy issue that can arise in the e-mail context is unauthorized publication of private correspondence. Publishing (that is, making available to others) an individual's e-mail may constitute a violation of that person's right of privacy. The tort is known as the "public disclosure of private facts." It arises when someone forwards another person's e-mail to others without permission or posts the message on the Internet, where it would be available to the public at large.

The elements of a claim for public disclosure of private facts are that (1) the e-mail is disclosed to others, (2) the disclosure is made without a legally recognized excuse, (3) the matters contained in the e-mail are private and of no public concern, and (4) the disclosure would bring shame and humiliation to a person of ordinary sensibilities.[4]

Employees bringing lawsuits against their employers for invasion of privacy for monitoring e-mail have generally not met with much success.

In the case mentioned in the Introduction that involved Nissan,[5] the company won the lawsuit because its explicit e-mail policy prevented the employees from arguing they had an expectation of privacy in their messages.

Another case involved a class action brought by employees who alleged that the employer circumvented their passwords and read their e-mail. The employer engaged in monitoring even though it had led employees to believe their messages would be private. All of the messages monitored were work-related. The court refused to extend California's right of privacy to employee e-mail and dismissed the lawsuit.[6]

Finally, a federal court in Pennsylvania dismissed a wrongful termination lawsuit, finding that the employee, who had been fired for making disparaging remarks about his supervisor in e-mail, had no expectation of privacy in his messages. The employer was free to read the employee's e-mail, even though it had fostered an atmosphere that led the employee to believe his messages would be private.[7]

Constitutional Privacy Rights

Federal, state, and local government employees have the protection of the Fourth Amendment to the U.S. Constitution, which bars unreasonable searches and seizures. In addition, several states specifically recognize the right of privacy for public employees in their constitutions (Alaska, Arizona, California, Florida, Hawaii, Illinois, Louisiana, Montana, South Carolina, and Washington). Of these states, only California extends constitutional privacy rights to both public and private employees. The California Supreme Court, however, has refused to extend the state's constitutional privacy right to a private employee's e-mail communications at work.[8]

These additional privacy rights generally turn on the same considerations as those of the common-law right of privacy. In both, the central question is whether the employee had a reasonable expectation of privacy. In the context of online communications, several courts have ruled that employees do not have a reasonable expectation of privacy in the e-mail they create and receive at work.[9] This is particularly so when the employer has a written e-mail policy, which puts employees on notice that the system is only to be used for business purposes and that messages are subject to monitoring.

The Electronic Communications Privacy Act

When employees found their claims of invasion of privacy unavailing, they turned to an obscure amendment to the federal wiretap statute, the Electronic Communication Privacy Act of 1986 (ECPA).[10] One of the motivating forces for the amendment was a 1985 Congressional study that graphically described potential threats that new technology posed to citizen's civil liberties. Congress passed the ECPA in part to address deficiencies in individual privacy protections.

It remains unclear how the ECPA applies to computer networks operated by private businesses. However, the ECPA is likely to apply if the business's private network has the ability to send and receive messages over external networks such as the Internet. Given the unsettled nature of this area of the law, businesses should assume the ECPA applies to them and draft their computer use policies accordingly.

For purposes of our discussion, the ECPA is directed at preventing two types of conduct: (1) unauthorized interception[11] of electronic communications (including e-mail[12]), and (2) unauthorized retrieval[13] of electronic communications from some form of storage medium (such as hard disks and magnetic tapes).

Employees whose communications have been wrongfully intercepted or retrieved may bring a civil suit against the wrongdoer. This means that employers engaged in monitoring their employees' e-mail may be subject to a lawsuit for damages under the ECPA.

The Act has a number of exceptions to liability. The most important one for employers is if one of the parties to the communication consents to interception:

> It shall not be unlawful under [the ECPA] for a person . . . to intercept a wire, oral, or electronic communication . . . where one of the parties to the communication has given prior consent to such interception unless such communication is intercepted for the purpose of committing any criminal or tortious act in violation of the Constitution or laws of the United States or of any State.[14]

This exception is why most e-mail policies include a provision expressly granting the employer the right to monitor messages. Thus, even if the ECPA applies to your business, a policy that includes a monitoring right is likely to prevent liability for reviewing employee messages.

A Word About Monitoring

A recent survey by the Society for Human Resources Management found that approximately one-third of the 538 business executives polled engaged in some form of e-mail monitoring. In most instances, monitoring conducted by businesses falls into three categories: responsive, random, or continuous.

Responsive monitoring is conducted in response to a particular problem or complaint. An employee informs her supervisor that another employee is sending inappropriate jokes through the e-mail system. In response to the complaint, the employer monitors the employee's e-mail.

Random monitoring is random sampling of employee e-mail to ensure that content is in compliance with the business's established policies. In most cases, the sampling is hardly scientific; a supervisor merely selects a number of e-mail accounts for monitoring. Because the volume of e-mail in even a small business may be substantial, random monitoring is seldom effective in detecting inappropriate or unauthorized messages.

Continuous monitoring provides the greatest monitoring capability. Specialized computer software is used to automatically and continuously monitor every e-mail message sent or received within the business. The software is very sophisticated and is capable of distinguishing between a message containing a single instance of profanity and one that is replete with inappropriate language. In addition to detecting profane, sexually explicit, and racially offensive content, the software can also be configured to look for use of trade secrets and other proprietary information. If a message is detected that matches certain defined criteria, it is flagged and an MIS operator or supervisor is automatically contacted.

Minimizing Potential Liability for Monitoring

The protections afforded employers by a well-written e-mail policy can be unintentionally vitiated by the employer's subsequent conduct. In many instances, employers lead their employees to believe they have an expectation of privacy notwithstanding any written policy to the contrary. For example, the employer may provide users with unique accounts on the computer that can only be accessed by a secret password of their choosing (without explaining to the employee that the password is for security purposes, not to protect the employee's privacy).

Employers should consider these steps to minimize the likelihood of a claim of invasion of privacy or violation of the ECPA by an employee:

- Access employee files and messages only if there is a legitimate business reason to do so (for example, responding to a discovery request during a lawsuit or investigating a claim by one employee against another relating to an offensive or inappropriate e-mail message).
- Educate employees that e-mail is to be used only for business purposes and that personal use is prohibited. This prevents personal information (in which an employee may have a strong privacy interest) from even existing on your system.
- Do not engage in conduct that leads employees to believe they have an expectation of privacy notwithstanding the express language of your policy.
- Require employees to acknowledge in writing that their computer files and messages are subject to review by the company and that they have no expectation of privacy in anything they create or receive on the system.
- Carefully review all union and collective-bargaining agreements to determine if there are any contractual limitations on employee monitoring. Some agreements may give employees an expectation of privacy that they do not normally have.

SAMPLE CLAUSES

No expectation of privacy. The computers and computer accounts given to users are to assist them in the performance of their jobs. Users should not have an expectation of privacy in anything they create, store, send, or receive on the computer

system. The computer system belongs to the company and may only be used for business purposes.
[*This clause and the following one are typically used together to directly address the issue of employee privacy.*]

Waiver of privacy rights. Users expressly waive any right of privacy in anything they create, store, send, or receive on the computer or through the Internet or any other computer network. Users consent to allowing personnel of the company to access and review all materials users create, store, send, or receive on the computer or through the Internet or any other computer network.
[*This broadly worded clause attempts to embrace everything an employee might create or receive on the computer.*]

No privacy in communications (alternative language). Users should never consider electronic communications to be either private or secure. E-mail could potentially be stored indefinitely on any number of computers, in addition to that of the recipient. Copies of your messages may be forwarded to others either electronically or on paper. In addition, e-mail sent to nonexistent or incorrect usernames may be delivered to persons that you never intended.
[*This is an example of a privacy clause that specifically focuses on electronic communications.*]

Monitoring of computer usage. The company has the right, but not the duty, to monitor any all aspects of its computer system, including, but not limited to, monitoring sites visited by users on the Internet, monitoring chat groups and newsgroups, reviewing material downloaded or uploaded by users to the Internet, and reviewing e-mail sent and received by users.
[*This is an example of an Internet-specific monitoring provision. It can be used alone or in combination with the general monitoring provision given above in the "Waiver of privacy rights" clause.*]

Automated monitoring. Users understand that the company may use automated software to monitor material created, stored, sent, or received on its computer network.
[*This clause notifies employees that the company is using specialized software to monitor traffic on its network.*]

Summary

Employee privacy rights in the online context should be a central issue in every computer use policy. A carefully drafted policy helps reduce employees' confusion concerning their privacy expectations and greatly reduces potential liability in the event of a dispute.

Endnotes

1. A common-law right is one developed by courts in the course of their decisions in various cases.
2. A *tort* is a civil wrong for which the injured party is entitled to damages against the wrongdoer.
3. Restatement (Second) of Torts, § 652B (1977).
4. *McNally v. The Pulitzer Publishing Co.*, 532 F.2d 69, 78 (8th Cir. 1976).
5. *Bourke v. Nissan Motor Co.*, (CA Super. Ct., 1991, docket no. YC 003979).
6. *Flanagan v. Epson America*, (CA Super. Ct., 1990, docket no. BC 007036).
7. *Smyth v. Pillsbury Co.*, 914 F. Supp. 97 (E.D. Pa. 1996).
8. *Flanagan v. Epson America.*, (CA Super. Ct., 1990, Docket No. BC 007036).
9. *Smyth v. Pillsbury Co.*, 914 F. Supp. 97 (E.D. Pa. 1996).
10. 18 U.S.C. §§ 2510-2710.
11. 18 U.S.C. § 2511(1)(a).
12. See for example *Steve Jackson Games Inc. v. U.S. Secret Service*, 36 F.2d 457 (5th Cir. 1994), finding that ECPA applied to e-mail.
13. 18 U.S.C. § 2701(a).
14. 18 U.S.C. § 2511(2)(d), relating to interceptions of electronic communications; see 18 U.S.C. § 2701(c)(2) relating to retrieval of stored electronic communications.

Chapter 3

Labor Organization Activities

When Can Employees Use Corporate Computers for Labor-Related Activities?

A business's computer system can greatly assist employees in performing their jobs. It can also serve as an important communication medium for employees to exchange information concerning labor organization. This is particularly true for large organizations, where employees may be spread out over a number of locations. The e-mail system or company computer bulletin board provides an easy and inexpensive means for employees to organize. Employers should be aware of this fact and tailor their computer use policies to address labor organizing activities online.

Labor Organizing by E-mail

When union organizing activities use the property of an employer, the employees' right to self-organization under Section 7 of the National Labor Relations Act (NLRA) must be weighed against the employer's property rights.[1] Section 7 provides that "employees shall have the right to self-organization, to form, join, or assist labor organizations."[2] Moreover, it is an unfair labor practice for an employer "to interfere with, restrain, or coerce employees in the exercise of rights guaranteed" in Section 7.[3]

Although an employer may not generally prohibit all organizing activities by employees, it may restrict the times and locations in which its facilities are used for organizing. In particular, employees do not have a statutory right to use their employer's computer system for any reason—personal or labor-organizational—other than to assist them in carrying out work-related duties. When an employer does, however, choose to permit employees to use business computer resources for nonwork-related activities (such as sending personal messages), Section 7 of the NLRA has been interpreted to require that the employer not discriminate against uses for labor organizing.[4]

For example, E. I. du Pont de Nemours & Co., allegedly had permitted employees to use e-mail for a wide variety of purposes, including personal use, that had nothing to do with the company's business. The administrative law judge in the case found that Du Pont had discriminatorily prohibited bargaining-unit employees from using the e-mail system for distributing union information, in violation of Section 8(a)(1) of the NLRA.[5]

As a result of Section 7, businesses should consider adopting computer use policies that limit use of corporate resources to business purposes only. Commercial or personal use of the computer system should be prohibited. Although a policy barring all personal use may seem unduly strict, the alternative may lead to unexpected and unwanted results.

Employee Use of E-mail for Protected "Concerted Activity"

Concerted activity is defined as action taken by a group of employees for the furtherance of their common interests. Section 7 of the NLRA protects employees who engage in concerted activities either for the purpose of collective bargaining or for mutual aid or protection. Thus, even without union involvement, employees cannot be terminated because they have gathered together to further some mutual interest with regard to their employment.

In one of the first cases involving concerted activity in the online environment, an employee was terminated because he refused to apologize for an e-mail he sent to fellow employees that was highly critical of a revision to the company's vacation policy. The National Labor Relations Board concluded that the employee's e-mail constituted "concerted activity" protected under Section 7 of the NLRA. In particular, the board found that the employee was attempting to address confusion over the revised vacation policy and to solicit his coworkers to pre-serve the existing policy, which would benefit all employees. The board ordered that the employee be reinstated immediately.

The outcome in this case might have been different if the employer had an explicit e-mail policy in place that strictly limited the use of corporate e-mail to business purposes only. With such a policy, an employer may be able to take action against employees who use the e-mail system for unautho-rized personal and labor-related activities. Unfortunately, most companies, whether they have a formal e-mail policy or not, allow some personal use of their e-mail system.

SAMPLE CLAUSES

Allowed use of computer system. The computer system is the property of XYZ Corporation and may be used only for legitimate business purposes. Users are permitted access to the computer system to assist them in the performance of their jobs. All users have the responsibility to use computer resources in a professional, ethical, and lawful manner. Use of the comput-er system is a privilege that may be revoked at any time.
[*This clause limits use of the computer system to legitimate busi-ness purposes only and does not allow for any personal use.*]

Allowed use of computer system (alternative language). The computer system is the property of XYZ Corporation and may only be used of approved purposes. Users are permit-ted access to the computer system to assist them in the per-formance of their jobs. Occasional, limited, appropriate personal use of the computer system is permitted when the use does not (1) interfere with the user's work performance; (2) interfere with any other user's work performance; (3) have undue impact on the operation of the computer system; or (4)

violate any other provision of this policy or any other policy, guideline, or standard of XYZ Corporation. At all times, users have the responsibility to use computer resources in a professional, ethical, and lawful manner. Personal use of the computer system is a privilege that may be revoked at any time.
[*This clause recognizes that certain personal uses are allowed, but that the uses must not interfere with the operation of the business. This type of clause should be considered carefully. Allowing any personal use of the computer system may prevent the company from discriminating against certain message content (for example, union-organizing activities).*]

Prohibited uses. Without prior written permission from _____, XYZ Corporation's computer system may not be used for dissemination or storage of commercial or personal advertisements, solicitations, promotions, destructive programs (that is, viruses or self-replicating code), political material, or any other unauthorized use.
[*It is sometimes helpful to specifically identify the type of use that is prohibited.*]

Summary

At present, there are only a handful of cases that have considered the implications of employee use of e-mail for labor-related activities. A business's best protection is to adopt a computer use policy that specifically defines the uses to which the computer system may be put. In addition, the business should carefully police the system to ensure that it is being used for only authorized activities.

Endnotes

1. Section 7 of the NLRB can be found at 29 U.S.C. § 157. See *Republic Aviation Corp. v. NLRB,* 324 U.S. 793 (1945), where employers must tolerate some use of their property to accommodate the self-organization rights of their employees.
2. 29 U.S.C. § 157.

3. 29 U.S.C. § 158(a)(1).
4. See for example *Roadway Express, Inc. v. NLRB*, 831 F.2d 1285, 1290 (6th Cir. 1987); an employer may not discriminate against union or other organizing material if it has chosen to allow personal messages on a company bulletin board; and *Central Vermont Hospital*, 288 N.L.R.B. 684 (1988).
5. 311 N.L.R.B. 88 (1993).

Chapter 4

Discrimination and Harassment

Avoiding a Hostile Work Environment

In increasing numbers, employers are finding themselves embroiled in employee disputes arising out of inappropriate or offensive content in e-mail. Racially or sexually oriented jokes and cartoons have already been the basis for a number of substantial lawsuits.

In one case, two African-American employees filed a discrimination lawsuit against their employer and several other employees based, in part, on repeated dissemination of allegedly racist jokes in e-mail.[1] The plaintiffs sought $5 million in compensatory damages and $25 million in punitive damages.

Because an employers is able to access and monitor employees' online communications, it may have a duty to protect employees from discriminatory or harassing material. The more carefully an employer monitors and controls online communications, the more likely it will be held liable if it fails to detect and remedy inappropriate content. Employers must take immediate corrective action when they learn of discriminatory or harassing messages.[2]

Since sexual harassment is the most prevalent form of discrimination involving e-mail, we focus our discussion on that area of the law. The principles, however, are generally the same for other forms of discrimination.[3]

Sexual Harassment: An Overview

Title VII of the Civil Rights Act of 1964 provides that it is "an unlawful employment practice for an employer . . . to discriminate against any individual with respect to his compensation, terms, conditions or privileges of employment, because of such individual's race, color, religion, sex or national origin."[4] In 1980, the Equal Employment Opportunity Commission prepared guidelines specifying that sexual harassment is a form of sex discrimination prohibited by Title VII of the Civil Rights Act.

Sexual harassment comes in many forms, but it generally involves physical or emotional pressure on an employee based on his or her gender. The two most common forms of harassment are quid pro quo and hostile environment.

Quid pro quo harassment arises when a supervisor or manager trades sexual favors with an employee in exchange for advancement in the company, when employment decisions are based on responses to sexual advances, and when retaliation is threatened if an employee refuses to respond to an advance. In one case, a supervisor in a well-known corporation sent e-mail messages that were offensive to women. After one women was not promoted, she sued for discrimination. The court found that the e-mail was evidence from which a reasonable jury could conclude that the reason for not promoting the woman was gender-based.[5]

The second type of harassment is a hostile work environment. This type of environment is present, and thus Title VII is violated, "when the workplace is permeated with discriminatory intimidation, ridicule and insult . . . that is sufficiently severe or pervasive to alter the conditions of the victim's employment and create an abusive work environment . . . ."[6] To bring a discrimination lawsuit based on a hostile work environment, the victim is not required to prove that employment decisions were influenced by the intimidation or harassment. This area of the law is directed at protecting the employee's right to "work in an environment free from discriminatory intimidation, ridicule and insult."[7]

In addition to federal statutes such as Title VII, there may also be potential liability for harassment under various state laws. For example, Arizona, California, Indiana, Michigan, New Hampshire, and Wyoming have all amended their harassment and stalking laws to include e-mail communications.[8]

Employer Liability for Sexual Harassment

Employers can be directly or indirectly liable for sexual harassment. Direct liability means the harassment is committed by the employer's supervisory employees or authorized agents, under the theory that the wrongful conduct should be imputed to the employer because it is responsible for their actions. More likely, however, the employer is held indirectly liable for failing to adequately address and correct behavior that creates a hostile work environment.

In the e-mail context, a hostile work environment may be created if e-mail is repeatedly circulated that contains sexually explicit language or jokes. An employer who becomes aware of this activity and fails to take immediate corrective action may very well find itself the subject of a lawsuit under Title VII.

It should be emphasized that a single offensive or inappropriate e-mail is probably not sufficient in and of itself to form the basis for a claim of hostile work environment. To constitute such an environment, the wrongful conduct must be severe and cannot consist of isolated incidents.[9] A federal court recently used this reason to dismiss a racial discrimination claim arising out of the circulation of a single piece of e-mail that was alleged to contain an offensive joke.[10]

The potential for a claim of discrimination cannot be entirely avoided by a computer use policy. Employees must be educated and sensitized as to what is and is not appropriate office conduct. They must understand their duty to avoid discriminatory activity and to immediately report such activity if they encounter it. The computer use policy merely formalizes these duties.

SAMPLE CLAUSES

Prohibited activities. Material that is fraudulent, harassing, embarrassing, sexually explicit, profane, obscene, intimidating, defamatory, or otherwise unlawful or inappropriate may not be sent by e-mail or other form of electronic communication (such as bulletin board systems, newsgroups, or chat groups) or displayed on or stored in XYZ Corporation's computers. Users encountering or receiving this kind of material should immediately report the incident to their supervisors.

[*This is an example of a catch-all clause defining inappropriate content for e-mail. This clause can be expanded or refined to address particular areas of concern. For example, language could be included to address off-color or discriminatory jokes or cartoons.*]

Disclaimer of liability for use of the Internet. XYZ Corporation is not responsible for material viewed or downloaded by users from the Internet. The Internet is a worldwide network of computers that contains millions of pages of information. Users are cautioned that many of these pages include offensive, sexually explicit, and inappropriate material. In general, it is difficult to avoid at least some contact with this material while using the Internet. Even innocuous search requests may lead to sites with highly offensive content. In addition, having an e-mail address on the Internet may lead to receipt of unsolicited e-mail containing offensive content. Users accessing the Internet do so at their own risk.

[*Use of the Internet falls under the category of caveat emptor ("let the buyer beware"). Even with the best filtering software, it is not always possible to avoid coming into contact with offensive content on the Internet. This clause makes clear that the company cannot protect employees from encountering this type of material.*]

Summary

As online communications become an ever more integral part of every business, employers must be sensitive to the possibility that this new medium is exploited for harassment and discrimination. Employers who fail to act to address this potential problem do so at their peril.

Endnotes

1. *Owens and Hutton v. Morgan Stanley & Co., Inc.*, Case No. 96 Civ. 9747 (S.D.N.Y. 1996). For reasons discussed below, the discrimination portion of the complaint was later dismissed. See also *Peterson v. Minneapolis Community Development Agency*, 194 Minn. App. LEXIS 834 (Aug. 23, 1994), where an employee discontinued physical contact with another employee after she complained but continued harassing her by e-mail; and *Strauss v. Microsoft Corp.*, 814 F. Supp. 1186 (S.D.N.Y. 1993), where a supervisor sent inappropriate e-mail to female employees, and the e-mail was taken as evidence from which a reasonable jury could find that failure to promote a woman was based on gender).
2. *Garziano v. E. I. du Pont de Nemours & Co.*, 818 F.2d 380 (5th Cir. 1987).
3. It should be noted that extreme cases of e-mail harassment can be treated as hate crimes and prosecuted criminally. The first federal trial involving hate e-mail was held in 1997, involving a message threatening to "hunt down and kill" Asian students at the Irvine campus of the University of California. See "Trial of Ex-Student Accused in Hate E-mail Case Begins," Los Angeles Times (Nov. 5, 1997).
4. 42 U.S.C. § 2000e2(a)(1).
5. *Strauss v. Microsoft Corp.*, 814 F. Supp. 1186 (S.D.N.Y. 1993).
6. *Harris v. Forklift Systems*, 510 U.S. 17 (1993).
7. Meritor Savings Bank v. Vinson, 477 U.S. 57 (1986).
8. Ariz. Rev. Stat. Ann. Supp. § 13-2921; Cal. Civ. Proc. Code § 527.8; Ind. Code Ann. Supp. § 35-45-2-2; Mich. Comp. Laws Ann. Supp. § 750.411i(1)(f); N.H. Rev. Stat. Ann. § 644:4; Wyo. Stat. Ann. § 6-2-506.
9. See *Tomka v. Seiler Corp.*, 66 F.3d 1295 (2d Cir. 1996).
10. *Owens and Hutton v. Morgan Stanley & Co.* (SDNY 7/17/97).

Part III

POTENTIAL CLAIMS BY THIRD PERSONS

Chapter 5

Copyright

Think Before You Cut and Paste

Use of e-mail poses two potential copyright issues. First, incorporating copyrighted material into e-mail without authorization is a violation of the federal Copyright Act. Second, the e-mail itself is subject to copyright. Copying or forwarding a message may constitute copyright infringement.

Federal copyright law is derived from language in the U.S. Constitution: Congress has power to "promote the progress of science and the useful arts, by securing for limited times to authors and inventors the exclusive right to their respective writings and discoveries."[1] To be eligible for copyright under the current Copyright Act, a work must be (1) original and (2) fixed in some tangible medium of expression (written on a piece of paper, recorded on an audiotape, stored in computer memory).[2]

The author of a copyrighted work has the exclusive right to do the following:

1. Make copies of the work.
2. Make other works based on the copyrighted work.
3. Distribute the work to the public.
4. In the case of certain works, to perform the work publicly.
5. Display the work to the public.
6. In the case of a sound recording, perform the work publicly by transmitting it digitally over a computer network.[3]

Anyone who infringes one of these exclusive rights can be sued for damages and enjoined from engaging in further infringing conduct.[4] In addition, the court may order the destruction of any physical objects that embody infringing material.[5] If the infringement was done for commercial advantage or personal financial gain, the infringer may also be subject to criminal prosecution.[6]

There are two theories under which a business may be held liable for copyright infringement committed by its employees or agents. First, the business may be held vicariously liable if it could have controlled the infringer and directly benefited financially from the infringement. A business may be found vicariously liable even though it has no knowledge of the infringing activity. Second, the business can be held contributorily liable by knowingly assisting in the infringing activity (for example, providing the computer system over which the copyrighted material is transmitted).[7]

Copyright in the Online Environment

Almost everything encountered online is protected by copyright. Text, sounds, pictures, programs, cartoons, jokes, and movies stored in electronic form are all potentially copyrightable.[8] Copying this material and incorporating it into a piece of e-mail is likely to infringe one or more of the copyright owner's exclusive rights.

All of these commonplace activities probably constitute copyright infringement:

- You copy the latest *Dilbert®* cartoon from the Internet and send it to a friend as an attachment to an e-mail.
- While perusing the *New York Times* Website, you find an interesting article on e-mail policies. You copy a paragraph from the article into an e-mail and send it to every manager in your company.
- You subscribe to a monthly e-mail newsletter that discusses recent developments on Internet law. Each month you forward a copy of the e-mail newsletter to the manager of your risk management department.

- You decide to spice up your e-mail by including a digitized audio clip from the "Seinfeld" TV show.
- The most recent issue of *Newsweek* contains a fascinating article on Elvis sitings. You type two of the paragraphs from the article verbatim into an e-mail and forward it to a friend in Las Vegas.
- Your company purchases the latest version of a popular computer game. You decide to "share" the program with a friend by attaching it to an e-mail.[9]

Copying material from the Internet is a particularly hazardous activity. Because the Internet is virtually unregulated, copyright infringement is rampant. It is almost impossible to tell where material came from, whether the material is in the public domain, or (if it is not) who owns the rights to the material. Just because the operator of a Web site assures you that you have permission to copy something, don't believe it. Always check to make sure the operator really owns the rights to the material.

Copyright infringement is a strict liability offense. Even if you have the purest of intentions and firmly believe that the author of a particular work has specifically granted permission to copy the work, you may still be held liable for copyright infringement if it turns out that the alleged author is not the true copyright owner. The old adage to look before you leap is particularly applicable to copyright law.

Now, you may be thinking, "there's no way anyone will ever find out that I copied a *Dilbert* cartoon and sent it to a friend." Well, for the same reason that it is extremely easy to copy material stored electronically, it is becoming relatively easy for the owners of copyrights to detect whether their works have been wrongfully copied online. A growing number of businesses and trade organizations are beginning to use automated programs called "robots" or "spiders" to traverse the Web looking for unauthorized copies of copyrighted works.[10] These programs can automatically scan the Web for copyrighted text, graphics, audio, and even video. If an unauthorized copy is detected, the program reports the location to its owner. It will not be long before this technology reaches e-mail.

Sample Clauses

Compliance with applicable laws and licenses. In their use of the computer system, users must comply with all software licenses; copyrights; and all other state, federal, and international laws governing intellectual property and online activities.
[*This clause is frequently included in policies as a general reminder to employees of their legal obligations in using the computer system.*]

Misuse of software. Without prior written authorization from _____, users may not do any of the following: (1) copy software for use on their home computers; (2) provide copies of software to any independent contractors or clients of XYZ Corporation or to any third person; (3) install software on any of XYZ Corporation's workstations or servers; (4) download any software from the Internet or other online service to any of XYZ Corporation's workstations or servers; (5) modify, revise, transform, recast, or adapt any software; or (6) reverse-engineer, disassemble, or decompile any software. Employees who become aware of any misuse of software or violation of copyright law should immediately report the incident to their supervisors.
[*Unlike the foregoing general clause concerning compliance with applicable laws and licenses, this clause provides employees with a specific list of "don'ts" regarding use of software. Because of the growing number of software audits that are being conducted by trade organizations, many businesses are including specific clauses like this one in their computer use policies. An example of a stand-alone software use policy is in Appendix A..*]

Copying software (alternative 1). Much of the software on XYZ Corporation's computer system was purchased under a license agreement or is protected by federal copyright law. These licenses or copyrights restrict our right to make copies of the software and, ins some cases, restrict the ways in which the software can be used. Users may not make copies of any licensed or copyrighted software from our systems without prior written approval of _____. Violations may result in disciplinary action, including termination, and possible civil and/or criminal penalties.

[*This is a more concise and informal version of the preceding clause concerning illegal copying of software.*]

Illegal copying (alternative 2). Users may not illegally copy material protected under copyright law or make that material available to others for copying. User are responsible for complying with copyright law and applicable licenses that apply to software, files, documents, messages, and other material they wish to download or copy. Users may not agree to a license or download any material for which a registration fee is charged without first obtaining the express written permission of

_____.

[*This example goes beyond software to include all types of copyrighted or licensed material. This type of clause may be appropriate in instances where employees frequently copy content from other sources, such as the Internet, and include it in their e-mail.*]

Is My E-mail Copyrighted?

Another potential source of copyright liability involving e-mail is the content of the message itself. The instant you finish typing a message, the e-mail is protected under federal copyright law. There is no need to register the message with the Copyright Office in Washington. There is no need to put the copyright symbol © on the message. Although doing these things affords you certain additional advantages in litigation, they are not necessary to protect your copyright in the message.

If you send an e-mail to your accountant, you have implicitly granted her the right to make a copy of the message on her hard disk. Depending on the circumstances, you may also have given the accountant permission to forward the message to someone else. But, you have probably not granted her permission to forward your message to a wide number of people, or to post your message on the Internet, or to take a portion of your message and incorporate it into something else she is working on. In each of these situations, the accountant may have infringed your copyright and would be subject to a lawsuit for damages.

Summary

Copying and distributing copyrighted material without authorization from its owner may result in substantial liability and possible criminal prosecution. Employees should be very careful in copying material from third parties or off the Internet. Your computer use policy should clearly define each employee's obligation to avoid infringing the intellectual property rights of others.

Endnotes

1. Art. I, § 8, cl. 8 of U.S. Constitution.
2. 17 U.S.C. § 102(a).
3. 17 U.S.C. § 106.
4. 17 U.S.C. §§ 502, 504.
5. 17 U.S.C. § 503.
6. 17 U.S.C. § 506.
7. *Religious Technology Center v. Netcom*, 907 F. Supp. 1361 (DC N CA, 1995).
8. The types of works eligible for copyright protection include, but are not limited to, literary works, including computer software; musical works; dramatic works; pictorial, graphic, and sculptural works; motion pictures and other audiovisual works; sound recordings; and architectural works; 17 U.S.C. § 102(a).
9. See Chapter __<tf:find> for a discussion of the legal aspects of copying software.
10. Digimark Corporation and Headspace Inc. are two of the many companies providing software that searches the Web for copyrighted materials. BMI, the music licensing agency that represents 180,000 songwriters and music publishers, has developed a Web robot to make sure copyright holders are justly compensated for music played on the Web.

Chapter 6

Defamation

Can I Say That?

Whenever you make negative statements about a person or another business, you run the risk of being sued for defamation.[1] Not all negative statements, however, are actionable. Truthful statements are immune from liability as defamation. Other statements are mere opinion rather than fact and are less likely to support a claim of defamation. But false statements of fact may form the basis of a claim for damages by the defamed party. At its heart, the law of defamation is an effort to balance free speech rights under the First Amendment against the rights of victims of false, harmful communications.[2]

E-mail and other electronic communications (such as postings to bulletin boards and newsgroups) pose a particular threat of claims for defamation. The online environment provides the means of disseminating a defamatory statement almost instantly to an audience of thousands, if not tens or hundreds of thousands, of people—something that would be prohibitively expensive using traditional forms of communication. This potential for wide dissemination of a defamatory statement may significantly increase the amount of damages incurred by the injured party.

Because e-mail can be created and sent within seconds, there is no cooling-off period as there would be for traditional written communications that have to be dictated, typed, and reviewed before being sent. Users can send e-mail while in an aggravated or emotional state to "blow off a little steam" and make negative statements they will later regret.

Liability for Online Defamation

There are essentially two ways in which a business may be found liable for defamatory statements made by an employee in an electronic communication:

1. *Agency liability*. The employee may be seen as a spokesperson or agent of the company. In this case, the statements of the employee are imputed to the business. This is a particular problem with e-mail because it makes every employee with an e-mail account a de facto spokesperson for the company, whether authorized or not. Corporate e-mail is usually addressed with the employee's name followed by the name of the business (for example, john_doe@mybusiness.com). The form of the e-mail address strongly implies the employee is speaking on behalf of the company.
2. *Liability as disseminator of defamatory material*. As the provider of the computer system, the business may be held liable for disseminating the defamatory material. Liability generally turns on whether the business is found to be a "publisher" of the material or merely its "distributor."

Publishers of books, magazines, and newspapers have historically been deemed to have acquired knowledge of material provided by third parties through the process of editing and producing their publications. Because of this knowledge, publishers are deemed to have adopted the material as their own and are thus generally liable for republishing defamatory material.[3]

In contrast, distributors are those who merely deliver or transmit material provided by third parties. They usually exercise no editorial control over the content of the material disseminated. Distributors are generally not liable for defamatory material unless they know or have reason to know of the defamatory nature of the material.[4]

The greater the control a business has over the content of a communication, the more likely it will be found to be a publisher. For example, if a business operates a moderated online bulletin board system for its employees and customers to discuss its products, the business may be found liable as a publisher of any defamatory comments made on the board. This is exactly what happened in a well known case involving Prodigy Services Co.

Stratton Oakmont, a securities investment firm, sued Prodigy for defamatory statements by an unidentified user on Prodigy's popular financial bulletin board, "Money Talk." Because Prodigy moderated the board to ensure that content was "family-oriented," it was found to be a publisher and potentially liable for the defamatory statements.

The court's ruling in the Prodigy case left businesses that provide bulletin boards and other online communications with a strong disincentive to exercise any control or to monitor content, even when they might have a legitimate business reason to do so.

The Communications Decency Act to the Rescue?

The disincentive created by the Prodigy case, troubled Congress and led in part to the enactment of the Communications Decency Act, which was part of the Telecommunications Act of 1996. Section 230(c) of the decency act contains a "Good Samaritan" provision that shields interactive computer services from liability for defamation: "no provider or user of an interactive computer service shall be treated as the publisher or speaker of any information provided by an information content provider." Interactive computer services are defined in section 230(e)(2) as "any information service, system, or access software provider that provides or enables computer access by multiple users to a computer server, including . . . access to the Internet. . . ."

One of the specific goals of the Good Samaritan provision was to overrule the Prodigy case and any similar decisions treating interactive computer service providers and users as publishers of content that they did not create, merely because they restricted access to the content.

Although few courts have interpreted the Good Samaritan provision, it appears fairly clear that the protections apply to computer systems operated by businesses for the use of their

employees. The Communications Decency Act should, there-
fore, provide a level of protection for employers against liability for defamatory comments made by their employees online.
But the protection does not provide blanket immunity from liability. An employer can still be held liable for an employee's
statements in certain situations, for example, if the employer is
aware of the defamatory material and transmits it anyway, or if
the employee is acting at the direction of the employer.

SAMPLE CLAUSE

Prohibited activities. Material that is fraudulent, harassing,
embarrassing, sexually explicit, profane, obscene, intimidating,
defamatory, or otherwise unlawful or inappropriate may not be
sent by e-mail or other form of electronic communication
(such as bulletin board systems, newsgroups, or chat groups) or
displayed on or stored in XYZ Corporation's computers. Users
encountering or receiving this kind of material should immediately report the incident to their supervisors.
[*This is an example of a catch-all clause defining inappropriate content for e-mail. This clause can be expanded or refined to address
particular areas of concern. For example, language could be included to address off-color or discriminatory jokes or cartoons.*]

Summary

Liability for defamation is a particular threat in electronic
communications. Employees must be educated to think before
they send messages. Sending an angry message without
reflection could lead to substantial liability for both employee
and employer.

Endnotes

1. *Defamation* is actually a catch term for two types of torts: libel
   (written statements) and slander (spoken statements). Although
   there has been much theoretical discussion about whether e-mail

and other online communications are "written" or "spoken," the difference is not particularly relevant for purposes of our discussion.
2. See for example *New York Times Co. v. Sullivan*, 376 U.S. 254 (1964).
3. *Cubby v. CompuServe* 776 F. Supp. 135 (S.D.N.Y. 1991).
4. *Stratton Oakmont, Inc. v. Prodigy Services Co.*, (N.Y. Sup., May 25, 1995).

Chapter 7

Spamming

Too Much of a Good Thing

Antispamming laws have become the center of attention in Congress and many state legislatures. Many people feel unsolicited commercial e-mail is almost a demonic presence; lawmakers have taken up the cause and appear determined to eliminate the "scourge." In addition, spammers are finding themselves the subject of a growing number of lawsuits. Many online service providers are suing spammers for damages for trespass, conversion, and even violation of the federal Computer Fraud and Abuse Act. Those who continue to send unsolicited commercial e-mail do so at their peril.

Potential Business Interruption

In addition to potential legal liability, spamming may result in substantial disruption to your business. Spamming begets spamming. Businesses that send unsolicited e-mail or make commercial postings to newsgroups may violate "netiquette" (an unwritten code of behavior for online users) and thus incur the wrath of the Internet community.

A few years ago, a business decided to send out voluminous e-mail and make postings on several newsgroups to promote its services. The Internet community viewed this activity as a breach of netiquette and instituted a spam attack on the business. Tens of thousands of e-mail flooded the business's Internet address. Thousands of pages of protest faxes clogged its facsimile machines, and hundreds of autodial telephone calls were made to its central switchboard. These acts virtually shut the business down for several days.

No More Spoofing

The experience of that business has led spammers to routinely disguise or "spoof" their return addresses and identities. Spoofing's days, however, are probably numbered. America Online recently filed a successful lawsuit against Cyber Promotions (the king of spammers), compelling it to stop using fake domain names and return addresses in its e-mail. In addition, spoofing is the subject of several proposed laws currently under consideration by Congress. These laws will impose fines on businesses that disguise their identity in unsolicited e-mail.[1]

States have also been active in the area of spoofing. For example, a new California law requires businesses offering goods or services for sale through the Internet or other means of electronic communication to reveal their identity and address. Violations of this requirement are punishable by up to six months in jail and fines of up to $1,000.[2]

A number of spoofing cases are making their way through the courts. In one of the first, a Texas court ordered a spammer to pay $18,900 in damages to the owner of a domain name that the spammer forged as the return address on its mass mailings. The judge ruled that the spoofing constituted a common-law nuisance and trespass. The judge also ordered the spammer not to use "any Internet domain name without the express written permission of the owner and administrator of that Internet domain name."[3]

SAMPLE CLAUSES

Sending unsolicited e-mail ("spamming"). Without the express permission of their supervisor, users may not send unsolicited e-mail to persons with whom they do not have a prior relationship. [*Spamming may result in substantial liability to the company. The computer use policy should include a clause specifically addressing* *this issue. If your particular state, or one of the states in which you do business, has a specific antispam law, this clause should be tailored to parallel the language of the statute.*]

Spoofing. Users may not, under any circumstances, use "spoofing" or other means to disguise their identities in sending e-mail. [*Spoofing is frequently used to hide the identity of a spammer or of someone who is committing unauthorized or illegal acts online. This practice generally has no application in the business environment and is usually forbidden.*]

Altering attribution information (alternative language). Users must not alter the "From:" line or other attribution-of-origin information in e-mail, messages, or postings. Anonymous or pseudonymous electronic communications are forbidden. [*This is a slightly broader version of the preceding antispoofing clause.*]

Summary

Businesses must be sensitive to the growing backlash against spammers. Sending unsolicited commercial e-mail may not only violate state and federal law but also cause a public relations nightmare for your company. Employees should understand and comply with the antispam laws for every jurisdiction in which they are sending e-mail.

Endnotes

1. See for example Senate Bill 771, introduced by Frank Murkowski (R-Alaska).
2. Cal. Bus. & Prof. Code § 17538.
3. "Put a Spammer in the Slammer, and Other Good Works," *PC Week* (Dec. 1, 1997).

Part IV

PROTECTING CORPORATE INFORMATION AND RESOURCES

Chapter 8

Trade Secrets and Other Confidential Information

Protecting Your Business's Most Valuable Assets

In today's information-based economy, trade secrets can be extremely valuable assets. Because trade secrets have value only because they are not generally known, businesses must take reasonable precautions to ensure their secrets are not revealed to the public or their competitors. Protecting trade secrets is a particular problem when they are stored on computers from which they can easily be copied and disseminated. There are two primary concerns:

1. An employee, intentionally or inadvertently, reveals a trade secret through an online communication (e-mail or a posting to a newsgroup).
2. An employee uses online communications to steal a trade secret for his or her own financial benefit.

These concerns have led many companies to adopt strict guidelines concerning use of trade secret information in e-mail and other electronic communications. For example, the president of Boeing Commercial Aircraft Group recently sent a memo to all employees reminding them that the Internet is a medium for external communication and that it should not be used to discuss Boeing's trade secret information without prior authorization.[1]

What Is a "Trade Secret," and Why Are
Trade Secrets Important?

It is a difficult task to provide a generic definition of *trade secret*. Many states and the federal government have their own unique definitions. For our purposes, however, the definition provided in the Uniform Trade Secrets Act (UTSA) is sufficient. With only slight modifications, this is the definition used by most states. The UTSA defines a trade secret as:

> Information, including a formula, pattern, compilation, program, device, method, technique, or process, that:
> (i) derives independent economic value, actual or potential, from not being generally known to, and not being readily ascertainable by proper means by other persons who can obtain economic value from its disclosure or use, and
> (ii) is the subject of efforts that are reasonable under the circumstances to maintain its secrecy.[2]

Stated less formally, a trade secret is generally (1) novel information, ideas, or methods that (2) are the subject of reasonable efforts under the circumstances to maintain relative secrecy and (3) are valuable because they are not generally known.

It is important to note that absolute secrecy is not required. The information need only be "relatively secret." This means that under certain circumstances you can maintain a trade secret even though other businesses have learned the secret, through independent development or misappropriation, as long as the information has not become generally known.

If someone misappropriates one of your trade secrets, you have a number of remedies. You can recover damages, which include your actual losses caused by the misappropriation as well as any unjust profits realized by the wrongdoer. You can also request that the court issue an injunction preventing the wrongdoer from continuing to exploit your trade secret. If there is evidence that the wrongdoer acted intentionally and willfully, the court may also award punitive damages.

These remedies, however, are not available if your information loses its trade secret protection because it has been revealed to third parties. As mentioned above, this is a particular danger when trade secrets are stored on computers and can be copied and disseminated with ease. Trade secret status may be lost in these typical circumstances:

- E-mail containing trade secrets is accidentally sent to the wrong party.
- E-mail containing trade secrets is intentionally sent to a competitor.
- Trade secrets are posted on an Internet newsgroup or Web site discussion group.

Already, there has been at least one instance in which trade secret protection was lost because confidential information was made available on the Internet. In that case, closely guarded, previously unpublished teaching materials of the Church of Scientology lost their status as trade secrets because they had "escaped into the public domain and onto the Internet." The documents had become "generally known" and were no longer protectible as trade secrets.[3]

Do I Have Trade Secrets?

There is an erroneous perception by many businesses that trade secrets are only an issue for large corporations or software developers. In reality, almost every type of business has information meriting trade secret protection.

Although this area of the law is constantly changing, numerous subjects have all been recognized as eligible for trade secret protection: computer programs, chemical formulas, blueprints for products, methods of manufacturing, certain types of databases, customer lists, technical data, and pending patent applications.

Whether a particular piece of information is a trade secret depends on a number of factors:

- The measures taken to protect the secrecy of the information
- Whether the information is generally known by other businesses
- The value of the information to the owner and its competitors
- The time and money spent to develop the information

Theft of Trade Secrets: A Growing Problem

Theft of trade secrets has become a booming industry. U.S. companies estimated that in 1992 they lost $1.8 billion from theft of trade secrets. A 1993 study by the American Society for Industrial Security found a 260% increase in the theft of proprietary information since 1985. Two recent studies estimate our economy now loses $2 billion per month from economic espionage.

E-mail has already figured prominently in several major lawsuits involving theft of trade secrets.

In one of the first cases of its kind, a vice-president of Borland International, a software developer, used e-mail to transmit alleged trade secrets and other proprietary information to Symantec Corporation, a direct competitor of Borland's. The vice-president later resigned from Borland, to immediately join Symantec. Borland sued Symantec for unfair competition.

More recently, Software maker Avant! Corp. faced potential criminal prosecution for theft of trade secrets from its competitor, Cadence Design Systems. Prosecutors say the case is one of the most blatant in the history of Silicon Valley. Several of Cadence's top employees left to create Avant! In September 1994, still another employee moved there from Cadence, and subsequent investigation revealed that this employee allegedly e-mailed four critical files containing trade secrets to his home computer before leaving. In April 1997 six Avant! managers were charged with theft of trade secrets and conspiracy.[4]

In an unusual case, a computer program used e-mail to automatically report that it had been stolen. A developer at Sun Microsystems was in the process of debugging a new computer program used by engineers to check the integrated circuits in Sun's products. The developer had included a tracking feature in the program that records the names and e-mail addresses of anyone who uses it. The feature was not included to protect trade secrets but rather to identify people at Sun who had used the software so that they could be interviewed about its performance. An employee allegedly took an unauthorized copy of the program with him when he quit to join ZSP, a startup company that designs digital signal processing equipment. When employees at ZSP allegedly used the program, they did not notice that it "phoned home" to report the use. The developer at Sun checked the log for the program and noticed that it had been used by people with e-mail addresses at ZSP. Sun sued for theft of trade secrets.

New Law Imposes Criminal Penalties for Theft of Trade Secrets

Legislation recently signed into law may provide a powerful weapon against trade secret theft. On October 11, 1996, President Clinton signed into law the Economic Espionage Act of 1996 (EEA), which imposes criminal liability on anyone who intentionally steals a trade secret. A bill proposing a civil version of the EEA that allows businesses to bring a federal lawsuit for trade secret theft is expected to be introduced in Congress in the near future.

An important aspect of the EEA is that it has refined the definition of *trade secret* to focus specifically on information stored on electronic media: "all forms and types of financial, business, scientific, technical, economic, or engineering information, including patterns, plans, compilations, program devices, formulas, designs, prototypes, methods, techniques, processes, procedures, programs, or codes, whether tangible or intangible, and whether or how stored, compiled, or memorialized physically, electronically, graphically, photographically, or in writing. . . ."

Violations of the EEA by foreign individuals can result in fines up to $500,000 or imprisonment for up to fifteen years, or both. Foreign organizations may be fined up to $10 million for violations of the EEA. For general trade secret theft, individuals can be fined up to $250,000 or imprisoned for up to ten years, or both; organizations can be fined up to $5 million. In addition to the sentence imposed, violators may be forced to forfeit to the United States any property or proceeds resulting from the violations or used in connection with the violations.

Summary

The key issue concerning trade secrets is whether they have been the subject of reasonable efforts under the circumstances to maintain relative secrecy. If secrecy has been compromised, the protections afforded trade secrets may be lost. The threat of compromise is of particular concern when trade secrets are included in electronic communications. Your computer use policy should remind employees that it is everyone's duty to protect trade secrets from unauthorized disclosure.

SAMPLE CLAUSES

Communication of trade secrets. Unless expressly authorized by _____, sending, transmitting, or otherwise disseminating proprietary data, trade secrets, or other confidential information of the company is strictly prohibited. Unauthorized dissemination of this information may result in substantial civil liability as well as severe criminal penalties under the Economic Espionage Act of 1996.
[*Clauses of this type are frequently included in policies to raise the consciousness of employees concerning the importance of maintaining trade secrets and the penalties for illegally exploiting them.*]

Communicating confidential information (alternative language). Always keep in mind that e-mail and the Internet are public methods of communication. When you send information via e-mail or make it available on the Internet, there is always a possibility that the information will be viewed by unauthorized individuals. Never send confidential, proprietary, or trade secret information without first obtaining authorization from your supervisor. This type of information is a valuable asset of the company and each of us must make sure that it is protected from unauthorized disclosure.

[*This is a less formal version of the preceding clause.*]

Endnotes

1. "Boeing Warns Workers: Keep Company Secrets off the Net," (Tacoma, Wash.) *News Tribune* (Mar. 26, 1996).b
2. Uniform Trade Secrets Act §1(4) (1985).
3. *Religious Technology Center v. Lerma,* 897 F. Supp. 260 (E.D. Vir. 1995).
4. "A Nest of Software Spies?" *BusinessWeek* (May 19, 1997).

Chapter 9

Attorney-Client Communications Using E-mail

Are They Protected?

To save time and expense, a growing number of businesses are using e-mail to communicate with their outside attorneys. Among other things, these communications may contain comments regarding strategy in a pending litigation, amounts to offer or accept in settlement negotiations, potential initial public offerings, tax planning, and other highly confidential information. In general, communications with your attorney are protected under the attorney-client privilege from review by third parties. The question is whether this same protection applies if the communications occur online.

One of the cornerstones of the attorney-client relationship is confidentiality. The cloak of confidentiality ensures that clients feel free to speak candidly with their attorneys and fully disclose the facts of their cases. The confidentiality of their communications is guaranteed by two mechanisms. First, every attorney is under an ethical obligation to keep communications with clients confidential.[1] Second, the attorney-client privilege generally prevents information about these communications from being discovered in litigation and shields attorneys from having to testify about those communications.

Although the attorney-client privilege is defined differently from state to state, the following is a good working definition of the privilege: "The attorney-client privilege permits a client to refuse to disclose, and to prevent others from disclosing, a confidential communication between client and attorney."[2]

Duty of Confidentiality

A lawyer's ethical duty not to reveal client information[3] implies that a lawyer must have some certainty or reasonable expectation that a means of communication will maintain confidentiality. Although the American Bar Association's ethics panel has not yet decided whether e-mail communications violate a lawyer's duty not to reveal client information, several state bar associations have considered the issue. For example, the North Dakota and Illinois state bar associations have ruled that lawyers may use unencrypted e-mail to communicate about routine matters with their clients unless unusual circumstances warrant increased security measures.[4] However, in unusual circumstances involving communications of highly sensitive information, use of e-mail without additional security such as encryption may not be appropriate.

Communicating With Your Attorney Online

The key element in every definition of the attorney-client privilege is the requirement that the communication be "confidential." If the communication is not confidential, if it is revealed to unnecessary third parties, the privilege may be lost. Communicating with your attorney using e-mail raises a number of questions in this regard:

- Are messages sent over a public network such as the Internet "confidential"?
- Should attorney-client e-mail be encrypted?
- Is the privilege lost if an attorney-client e-mail is misaddressed and received by a third party?
- Is the privilege lost if a message is unintentionally forwarded to unnecessary third parties?

- Is the privilege lost if a system error causes a message to be misdelivered to an unrelated third party?

Unfortunately, the answers to these questions remain unclear. Because use of e-mail in communicating with attorneys is still a relatively new phenomenon, few courts have had an opportunity to consider these issues.[5] However, we can expect courts to resolve these questions by focusing on whether the client showed an intent to keep the messages confidential. One aspect of the court's analysis is likely to be whether the client took or failed to take precautions to protect the confidentiality of the communications.[6]

If a communication is revealed by a genuine mistake and there is little evidence the client was negligent in revealing the message, the privilege will probably be upheld. However, if there is evidence the client failed to act reasonably to protect confidentiality, the court may rule that the privilege was lost.

This brings us to an important question: If a public network is used to transmit attorney-client communications and those communications can be easily misaddressed or misdelivered, is it unreasonable not to use some form of encryption to protect messages from disclosure to unauthorized third parties? In other words, is failure to use encryption an indication that a client does not intend to keep messages confidential? If a court answers either of these questions in the affirmative, it may very well find that unencrypted messages are not protected by the attorney-client privilege. We will have to wait to see how courts resolve this issue. In the meantime, every business should consider encrypting its communications with attorneys to ensure they are not disclosed to unintended parties.

SAMPLE CLAUSES

Standard footers for e-mail. This footer should be appended to all e-mail sent outside the company:

> This e-mail and any files transmitted with it are confidential and are intended solely for the use of the individual or

entity to whom they are addressed. This communication may contain material protected by the attorney-client privilege. If you are not the intended recipient or the person responsible for delivering the e-mail to the intended recipient, be advised that you have received this e-mail in error and that any use, dissemination, forwarding, printing, or copying of this e-mail is strictly prohibited. If you have received this e-mail in error, please immediately notify _____ by telephone at _____. You will be reimbursed for reasonable costs incurred in notifying us.

[It is just as important in sending e-mail-as it is in sending facsimiles-to make sure that misdirected messages are handled properly. A footer similar to the type used on fax cover sheets should be included on every e-mail sent outside the company.]

Attorney-client communications. E-mail from or to in-house counsel or an attorney representing the company should include this warning header on each page: "ATTORNEY-CLIENT PRIVILEGED; DO NOT FORWARD WITHOUT PERMISSION." Communications from attorneys may not be forwarded without the sender's express permission.
[Communications with counsel should always be handled with the utmost care. If a message falls into the wrong hands, it may result in waiver of the attorney-client privilege. Including an appropriate header on all attorney-client communications is an important step in protecting the privilege.]

Summary

Communications with your attorney are generally protected by the attorney-client privilege. To ensure this protection extends to your e-mail communications with counsel, you should take reasonable measures to confirm that messages are correctly addressed, that messages are not forwarded to unnecessary parties, and that messages are clearly identified as attorney-client communications. For additional security, you should consider encrypting all attorney-client messages.

Endnotes

1. Model Code of Professional Responsibility, Rule 1.6.
2. See for example Cal. Evid. Code § 954; *United States v. Moscony*, 927 F.2d 742, 751 (3d Cir. 1991).
3. See for example Model Code of Professional Responsibility, Rule 1.6.
4. North Dakota State Bar Association Ethics Committee, Opinion 97-09, 9/4/97. The opinion of the Illinois Bar can be found at www.illinoisbar.org/CourtsBull/EthicsOpinions/96-10.html. See also South Carolina State Bar Opinion 97-8. South Carolina and Iowa, however, have both issued opinions concluding that, because it is possible for e-mail to be intercepted, it is an ethical violation for lawyers to send "sensitive" communications unless encrypted or unless the client specifically consents to the nonsecure method of communication. See South Carolina Bar Advisory Opinion 94-27 (Jan. 1995); Iowa Supreme Court Board of Professional Ethics and Conduct Opinion 96-1 (Aug. 29, 1997).
5. Some states, such as California, have adopted specific laws addressing the general issue of a client's use of electronic methods (fax machines, e-mail, cellular phones) to communicate with his or her attorney: "A communication between client and his or her lawyer is not deemed lacking in confidentiality solely because the communication is transmitted by facsimile, cellular telephone, or other electronic means between the client and his or her lawyer." Cal. Evid. Code § 952.
6. See for example *Hartman v. El Paso Natural Gas Co.*, 107 N.M. 679, 763 P.2d 1144 (1988), which identifies the reasonableness of precautions taken to prevent inadvertent disclosure as a factor in determining whether the attorney-client privilege has been lost.

Chapter 10

Computer Security

Protecting confidential, proprietary business information from disclosure and possible theft requires careful attention to network security. As mentioned above, the confidentiality of trade secrets and attorney-client communications is of particular importance. In addition to these areas, physicians, health care organizations, and brokers and other financial service providers all have obligations to maintain the confidentiality of client information. Unauthorized disclosure of such information could result in loss of trade secret status, forfeiture of the attorney-client privilege, and potential liability to third parties (clients and patients). This chapter provides an overview of several computer security issues that are relevant to computer and e-mail use policies.

Know Who Has Access to Your Computer System

In analyzing the security of any computer system, one of the most important considerations is the issue of who has access to the system and the information stored on it. Employees should understand their duty to preserve the security of their employer's network, to avoid accessing other networks and computers without permission, to refrain from accessing or modifying files without authorization, and to never tamper with the operation of the computer system or any of its files.

SAMPLE CLAUSES

Accessing other user's files. Users may not alter or copy a file belonging to another user without first obtaining permission from the owner of the file. The ability to read, alter, or copy a file belonging to another user does not imply permission to read, alter, or copy that file. Users may not use the computer system to "snoop" or pry into the affairs of other users by unnecessarily reviewing their files and e-mail.

[*This clause makes clear that employees may not access the files and e-mail of other users without a legitimate business reason to do so.*[1]]

Accessing other computers and networks. A user's ability to connect to other computer systems through the network or by a modem does not imply a right to connect to those systems or to make use of those systems unless specifically authorized by the operators of those systems.

[*Accessing unauthorized computers or networks within a company may compromise confidential or trade secret information. In the case of outside systems, unauthorized access may lead to criminal prosecution.*]

Computer security. Each user is responsible for ensuring that his or her use of outside computer and networks, such as the Internet, does not compromise the security of XYZ Corporation's computer network. This duty includes taking reasonable precautions to prevent intruders from accessing the company's network without authorization and to prevent introduction and spread of viruses.

[*Access to outside networks can create a security loophole. Employees should be aware of this problem and understand their duty to protect the company's computer system.*]

Computer security (alternative language). Users may not attempt to circumvent XYZ Corporation's data protection measures or uncover security loopholes or bugs. Users may not gain or attempt to gain unauthorized access to restricted areas or files on the computer system. Users should not tamper with any software protections or restrictions placed on computer applications, files, or directories. Users who engage in this type of activity may be subject to immediate termination.

[*This clause is directed at technically astute employees who may be tempted to tamper with or hack your computer system.*]

A Few Words About Passwords

Passwords generally have two purposes. First, they prevent unauthorized individuals from accessing a computer or a particular file. For example, trade secret information is usually password protected to limit its dissemination to only necessary employees. The other use of passwords is to link activities conducted on the computer with a particular user. In other words, if you log onto a computer or network using your password, everything you do while logged on can be traced to your account. This may be important for accounting purposes or to track who has accessed a particular file and when.

If an unauthorized third party steals or guesses a password, the security of your entire computer system may be compromised. To prevent possible theft of passwords, employees should avoid writing their passwords on paper, particularly paper located near their computers. Employees should also be careful to make sure no one is watching as they type their passwords into the computer. Hackers frequently visit businesses for apparently innocuous reasons for the sole purpose of trying to catch a password as it is typed into the system.

Employees must also use care in selecting their passwords. Passwords should not be based on personal information (birthday, address, telephone number, dog's name), that can easily be guessed. For greatest security, passwords should be at least six characters in length and a mix of uppercase and lowercase letters and special characters (e.g., Mm77$$, w86!!%%, MyPaSSwoRd).

SAMPLE CLAUSES

Responsibility for passwords. Users are responsible for safeguarding their passwords for access to the computer system. Individual passwords should not be printed, stored online, or given to others. Users are responsible for all transactions made using their passwords. No user may access the computer system using another user's password or account. Users may not disguise their identity while using the computer system.

[Even the best computer security system can be defeated if a user allows his or her password to be compromised. Every user should understand the duty to protect passwords.]

Password upkeep. Passwords should be obscure and a minimum of six characters in length. For best security, passwords should include both uppercase and lowercase and special characters (e.g., "@," "!," "&," "%"). All passwords must be changed every sixty (60) days. Users who do not change their passwords within the time prescribed may be automatically locked out of the system.

[A growing number of computer use policies include specific guidelines for ensuring password security.]

Passwords do not imply privacy. Use of passwords to gain access to the computer system or to encode particular files or messages does not imply that users should have an expectation of privacy in the material they create or receive on the computer system. XYZ Corporation has global passwords that permit it access to all material stored on its computer system-regardless of whether that material is encoded with a particular user's password. XYZ Corporation has the right to inspect, without prior notice, all material stored on its computer system.

[Although essential for security, use of passwords may lead employees to believe their work or messages will not be reviewed. This misperception should be specifically addressed in the policy.]

Encryption 101

The standard method of sending and receiving e-mail over the Internet, the one we all use, has almost no security features built into it and no capability for encryption. Anyone who comes into contact with a message can read it.

E-mail is susceptible to interception and review by unauthorized or unintended parties at numerous stages of communication. For example, a message can be read on the sender's hard disk, on the sender's network or its backup tapes, on intervening computers between the sender and recipient through which the e-mail is transmitted, on the recipient's hard disk, and the recipient's network or on its backup tapes.

Because e-mail is like an electronic postcard and can be viewed or intercepted in a number of ways, many businesses and individuals have started using encryption to provide a level of security for their communications. A discussion of encryption as it relates to use of e-mail and other online documents could easily fill an entire book. For our purposes, it is only important to understand some basic terminology.

Using encryption has two significant benefits. First, it prevents disclosure of sensitive information to unauthorized third parties. Second, encryption allows for "authentication" of the information sent. Authentication allows the recipient of the message to confirm that the message was actually sent by the sender, and not someone impersonating the sender, and that the message is genuine and has not been modified in anyway.

At its heart, encryption is a means of coding messages so they appear to be random characters. For example, the message "meet me Monday" may look like "#*%Mn yUj78#" when encrypted. The original message, "meet me Monday," is called the plaintext version of the message. The encoded message, "#*%Mn yUj78#," is called the ciphertext version of the message. Without an appropriate password, the message cannot be read once it is encrypted.

There are essentially two types of encryption in general use today: private key encryption and public key encryption. The primary difference is the number of passwords or "keys" that are used. Because it is more suitable for public networks, public key encryption is the encryption method of choice by most e-mail users.

Private key (symmetric) *encryption* uses only one secret password. The same secret password is used to encode and decode the message. An example of private key encryption would be the passwords used to encode word processing or spreadsheet files. An elementary form of private key encryption used on the Internet, particularly in newsgroups, is the ROT13 cipher. Basically, this code substitutes each letter of a message with the letter thirteen places away from it in the alphabet. For example, the message "hi" would encode to "uv."

In *public key* (asymmetric) *encryption*, every user has two passwords: (1) one that is secret and is never revealed to anyone, and (2) one that is public and is disseminated freely. The two passwords are mathematically related, but one cannot be derived from the other. Here is a simple example of how public key encryption is used. Smith wants to send Jones a secure e-mail. Smith asks Jones for his public key, which can be distributed freely and does not jeopardize the security of the message if it falls into the wrong hands. Smith encodes the message with Jones's public key and then sends the message to Jones. The message can only be decoded with Jones's secret key, which is known only to Jones. Jones's public key cannot decode the message.

Whether a business uses private key encryption or public key encryption, there are several potential pitfalls that employers should be aware of:

- Employees should only use encryption software approved by their employer.
- The employer should have a global or "back door" password permitting access to all encrypted files.
- Employees should understand that use of passwords should not create an expectation of privacy in the messages or files they encode.

The ability to access files encrypted by employees should be a very real concern for businesses. Files encoded with today's sophisticated encryption programs cannot be decoded even by law enforcement agencies. If there is no global access password and an employee refuses to reveal the password, it may be impossible to retrieve the encoded information. This problem recently arose at a well-known university. A librarian who believed she was going to be terminated refused to turn over the password for a critical database. Fortunately for the university, the information could be reconstituted from other sources. The lesson, however, is clear: Make sure you can access information encoded by your employees.

SAMPLE CLAUSES

Use of encryption software. Users may not install or use encryption software on any of XYZ Corporation's computers without first obtaining written permission from their supervisors. Users may not use passwords or encryption keys that are unknown to their supervisors.

[*This clause emphasizes the importance of using only company-supplied encryption software. The clause also makes clear that the company must have access to all passwords used to encode information on its system.*]

Use of encryption software (alternative language). Apart from login passwords, users may not use passwords or other encryption keys to prevent access to their work on the computer system. Users found to possess encrypted files are subject to disciplinary action and possible termination.

[*This clause may apply if the company does not permit use of any encryption software on its system.*]

Export restrictions. The federal government has imposed restrictions on export of programs or files containing encryption technology (such as e-mail programs that permit encryption of messages and electronic commerce software that encodes transactions). Software containing encryption technology is not to be placed on the Internet or transmitted in any way outside the United States without prior written authorization from _____.

[*This clause is frequently included to stress the importance of complying with U.S. restrictions, on export of encryption information. In most instances, employees violate export restrictions inadvertently, by not realizing a particular program contains encryption technology. If your company uses such programs, they should be specifically mentioned in this clause. Doing so alerts employees as to which programs pose potential export problems.*]

The Virus Problem

Simply clicking on an attachment to your e-mail or downloading a file from the Internet may result in severe damage to your computer system and possible catastrophic data loss. Viruses and other destructive programs cost businesses millions of dollars each year and have spawned a cottage industry of virus protection software companies. A recent study predicted that viruses will soon account for more than 60 percent of all security incidents.

Viruses come in all shapes and sizes. In addition to programs and executable files, word processing documents and spreadsheets can also contain viruses known as "macroviruses." The number of macroviruses spread from 40 in 1996 to more than 1,300 by November 1997.

Employees must understand how disks and files from outside the company are to be processed to minimize the potential for an infection. In many instances, employees do not consider their home computers a threat. But they are one of the primary sources of viruses. Home computers are used for many purposes, including surfing the Internet. Many people have access to them. Disks and files from home should be subject to the same scrutiny as any other outside material.

It is difficult to ensure that all employees have the latest version of virus checking software and, more importantly, know how to use it. This why many businesses have chosen to designate certain employees as "virus checkers." These employees, typically secretaries, receive specific training on the using virus checking software and serve as the entry point for loading outside material onto the business's network.

SAMPLE CLAUSES

Installation of software. Users may not install software onto their individual computers or the network without first receiving express permission from their supervisor.
[*This clause addresses two potential problems: installing software that may contain dangerous computer viruses, and, installing software that may not be properly licensed (that is, illegally copied software).*]

Virus detection. Viruses can cause substantial damage to computer systems. Each user is responsible for taking reasonable precautions to avoid introducing viruses into XYZ Corporation's network. To that end, all material received on floppy disk or other magnetic or optical media and all material downloaded from the Internet or from computers or networks that do not belong to XYZ Corporation MUST be scanned for viruses and other destructive programs before being placed onto our computer system. Users should understand that their home computers and laptops may contain viruses. All disks transferred from these computers to XYZ Corporation's network MUST be scanned for viruses.

[*Because viruses pose a substantial threat to computer systems, computer use policies should specifically detail the procedures employees use for handling disks or files from outside the company.*]

Virus detection (alternative language). Files obtained from sources outside the company, including disks brought from home; files downloaded from the Internet, newsgroups, bulletin boards, or other online services; files attached to e-mail; and files provided by customers or vendors, may contain dangerous computer viruses that can damage the company's computer network. Users should never download files from the Internet, accept e-mail attachments from outsiders, or use disks from noncompany sources without first scanning the material with company-approved virus checking software. If a user suspects that a virus has been introduced into the company's network, he or she should notify _____ immediately.

[*This alternative virus clause includes a notification provision.*]

Accessing the Internet. To ensure security and avoid the spread of viruses, users accessing the Internet through a computer attached to XYZ Corporation's network must do so through an approved Internet firewall[2] Accessing the Internet directly, by modem, is strictly prohibited unless the computer you are using is not connected to the company's network.

[*This clause reminds users that access to the Internet should only be made through an approved firewall and that using a direct-connect modem is to be avoided.*]

Ten Tips for Better Computer Security

The following tips are security necessities for every computer system:

1. Develop and implement a written security policy that applies to all aspects of employee computer use, including e-mail and Internet access.

2. Conduct regular employee training sessions to keep employees updated on company security practices.

3. Consider using "thin clients" (computers without hard disks or, in some cases, floppy drives) for employee computers. This type of computer makes it more difficult for employees to install games and other unauthorized software and to infect the business's network with viruses. Computers without disks also reduce the likelihood that critical information is left on employee's desks or, worse yet, stolen from the business.

4. Configure employee computers so that only one user ID is used per machine.

5. Always shred or burn confidential, sensitive business information (employee lists, user IDs, customer files, network documentation). External garbage bins are a common target for hackers, competitors, and those engaged in industrial espionage.

6. Use encryption to protect sensitive files and messages.

7. Keep network records updated. Promptly delete users who are no longer employees.

8. Configure your network to require users to change their passwords frequently. Educate users about the importance of creating passwords that are difficult to guess and to protect those passwords from inadvertent disclosure.

9. Regulate and control employee use of the Internet. Where appropriate, use monitoring and blocking software to prevent employees from accessing inappropriate and illegal material.

10. Install and frequently update virus protection software.

In addition, it is important to periodically review security-related resources on the Internet. These sources can provide early notice of new viruses and recently discovered network security concerns.[3]

Summary

Today, companies use computers for almost every aspect of their business. This reliance on computers has brought security concerns to the foreground. Businesses must take affirmative measures to ensure the integrity of their networks and the security of their sensitive communications.

Endnotes

1. Merely accessing another user's files and copying information from them without permission may constitute a crime in some states. See for example Cal. Pen. Code § 502 (Comprehensive Computer Data Access and Fraud Act).
2. A firewall is a software/hardware method of protecting a business's network from unauthorized access through the Internet.
3. See for example www.infowar.com/hackers, www.techbroker/happyhacker.html, and www.cert.org.

Chapter 11

Preventing Waste of Computer Resources

Employee waste of computer resources is a growing concern for business. Computer networks have finite bandwidth and limited storage capacity. Employee misuse and abuse of these resources may result in increased network traffic, slower response time for legitimate business activity, and increased costs for data storage. Employers must take reasonable precautions to ensure that the benefits derived from employee use of computers are not outweighed by several negative factors. These negative factors are the subject of this chapter.

Spamming

Junk e-mail sent to the e-mail addresses of employees at work has become an area of significant concern for employers.[1] Spam can overload network servers and cost money for storage. One large multinational corporation estimated it spends about one dollar per employee per day-approximately $55,000 daily-in costs directly related to handling spam.[2]

Spammers use sophisticated software that scans newsgroups, corporate Web sites, and other areas of the Internet for e-mail addresses to add to their mailing lists. These programs can quickly go through a business's Web site and collect the names and e-mail addresses of every employees. Given the minimal cost of sending mass e-mailings, it is easy to see how corporate networks are becoming clogged with junk mail. The problem is worsening as a growing number of spammers include graphics-intensive HTML files—which can include many megabytes of content-in their messages. Sending dozens of messages of this type to a business quickly creates a network bottleneck and consumes valuable storage capacity.

Businesses generally use a combination of two approaches to combat spam. First, filtering software is installed at the server or the firewall. This software uses a set of rules to identify and eliminate junk e-mail. For example, rules can be set up to block messages having toll-free 800 and 888, or toll-charge 900, telephone numbers in them, or messages containing sexually explicit language. Filtering can also block e-mail from particular domains known to be used by spammers.

The second approach is implemented at the user level. Most popular e-mail software, such as that bundled with Internet browsers, can be programmed to automatically delete messages based on these same types of rules. For messages that somehow make their way through these two levels of filtering, employees are urged to check the message to see if there is an e-mail address for requesting removal from the mailing list. If an address is given, employees are encouraged to send a removal request.

Legislative relief from spam may be on the way. Currently, a number of state legislatures and Congress are all considering proposed laws regulating spam. Until those laws are passed, however, businesses must rely on an aggressive filtering campaign for protection.

Listservers

An area related to spamming is listserv. A listserv is essentially an online discussion group conducted through e-mail. Users subscribe to a listserv that discusses a particular area of interest (environmental regulations, particle physics, Web marketing, a particular software program). Each list may have hundreds or even thousands of members. Sending an e-mail to the list automatically causes the message to be forwarded to every subscriber. During the course of a given day, subscribers may receive dozens, or more commonly hundreds, of messages from the listserv. To add to the volume of messages, it is not unusual for users to subscribe to more than one listserv.

An employee who subscribes to several listservs may single-handedly increases the volume of e-mail through the employer's server by as much as several hundred messages a day. If a significant number of employees subscribe to listservs, the increased e-mail traffic may seriously impact the performance of the business's network. For this reason, many employers prohibit employees from subscribing to listservs or limit their use to discussions that are directly relevant to the employee's job function.

Chain E-mail

Chain e-mail is a message sent to a number of people, asking each recipient to send copies with the same request to a specified number of others. The message may be sent as part of a get-rich-quick scheme or merely to propagate an amusing joke. Chain e-mail is growing ever more popular on corporate networks and is quickly becoming a substantial drain on their computer resources. The circulation of a chain letter increases in geometrical progression if the instructions are followed by all recipients. This can seriously degrade network performance and consume substantial amounts of valuable storage space. Initiating or forwarding chain e-mail serves no legitimate business purpose. The practice should be strictly prohibited.

Excessive Use of the Internet

Although the Internet is a powerful tool for conducting business, employee use of the Internet may result in potential problems:

- *Liability.* Material and messages sent to, or received from, the Internet by employees may give rise to liability on the part of their employer for defamation, harassment, copyright infringement, invasion of privacy, and discrimination.[3]

- *Loss of productivity.* The average employee spends three hours per week on nonbusiness-related Internet use. Recent surveys suggest that the number is significantly higher. This unnecessary Internet use also has adverse impact on the response time for other employees in attempting to use the Internet or their employer's internal network for legitimate business-related activities.
- *Increased costs.* Internet access is not without cost, and it consumes internal computing resources. For example, one large corporation saw 40 percent of the bandwidth for its Internet connection taken up by a handful of employees using a screen saver that was constantly updated through the Internet to display news and sports-related information. Another company found that 15 percent of the sites visited by its employees were sexually explicit.

Software is now available that can provide an enterprisewide means of addressing the problems that arise from employee use of the Internet. These programs fall into two categories: monitoring software and filtering (or blocking) software. Although firewalls, proxy servers, and routers provide a certain amount of monitoring and filtering, they generally cannot provide the level of sophistication and comprehensiveness found in dedicated software designed for this purpose.

Monitoring software maintains a log of "how" employees are using the Internet. The software generally examines the addresses of Websites visited, the types of files transferred (text, graphic, or audio), search engines used and searches performed, Internet protocols used (FTP, HTTP, SMTP) and the e-mail addresses to which messages are sent. In addition, the software can record which employee accessed the Internet on what date and at what time, and the duration of the access.

Merely posting summaries of Internet usage may be sufficient to prevent abuse of Internet access privileges. For example, one large financial institution installed monitoring software and posted weekly usage reports by department.[4]

Filtering software either limits employee access to only those Web sites and other Internet resources specifically identified on an "allowed list" or it allows access to everything that isn't identified on a "prohibited list." The business can create the lists itself or add to lists created by groups dedicated to rating Web sites and other Internet resources. Because the Internet is constantly changing, it is impossible to track every inappropriate site and block access. Consequently, most filtering software also includes rule-based blocking, which can be configured to prevent access to sites that contain sexually explicit language, games, or other key terms. Access to certain areas of the Internet can also be based on time of day. For example, the software might be configured to allow access to game and sports-related sites only before or after normal business hours.

Both monitoring and filtering software can be programmed to send a warning notice to employees who are using the Internet excessively or are attempting to gain access to inappropriate, nonbusiness-related material. The notice can inform the employees that they are in violation of corporate policy and that their use of the Internet is being logged. The software can also send an automated notice to the employee's supervisor or other designated manager.

Sample Clauses

Duty not to waste computer resources. Users must not deliberately perform acts that waste computer resources or unfairly monopolize resources to the exclusion of others. These acts include, but are not limited to, sending mass mailings or chain letters, subscribing to nonbusiness-related listservers and mailing lists, spending excessive amounts of time on the Internet, playing games, engaging in online chat groups, printing multiple copies of documents, or otherwise creating unnecessary network traffic.
[*Computer resources are not unlimited. There is finite bandwidth on the network and limited storage capacity. Employees should be aware of their duty to conserve these valuable resources.*]

Large file transfers. Users should schedule communications-intensive activities such as large file transfers, mass e-mailings, and streaming audio or video for off-peak times (that is, before

9:00 A.M. and after 4:00 P.M., Monday through Friday). Because audio, video, and picture files require significant storage space, files of this sort may not be downloaded unless they are business-related. All files that are downloaded must be scanned for viruses and other destructive programs.

[*This example attempts to reduce network traffic by scheduling certain activities during non-peak hours.*]

Conclusion

Waste of corporate computer resources is costing businesses millions of dollars each year in lost productivity, legal liability, and increased computing costs. To bring these losses and costs under control, employers should take three steps:

1. Adopt a written policy regarding waste of computer resources.
2. Educate employees about proper use of the computer and, in particular, the Internet.
3. Install appropriate monitoring and filtering software to prevent access to inappropriate content and to identify problem employees.

Endnotes

1. For more information about spam, see the Web sites www.spam.abuse.net, www.cert.org, and www.cauce.org.
2. "Junk E-mail Jangles Nerves," *LANTimes*, vol. 15, issue 3 (Feb. 2, 1998).a
3. See Parts II and III of this book.
4. "Managing Employee Internet Access: A Guide for Creating and Administering Corporate Access Policy with Monitoring and Filtering Software," Secure Internet Filtering Technology Consortium (Sept. 1997).

Part V

Putting It All Together: Constructing an E-Mail and Computer Use Policy

Chapter 12

Six Essentials for Every Good Policy

Computer and e-mail use policies can range from a few paragraphs to lengthy, multipage documents with exhibits. Regardless of the length and complexity of the policy, a handful of underlying principles should always be emphasized.

The Computer Belongs to the Business

The policy should make clear that the computer and e-mail systems belong to the business and are only to be used for authorized purposes. Employees should be cautioned against wasting computer resources or unfairly monopolizing resources to the exclusion of others. These acts include, but are not limited to, sending mass mailings or chain letters, spending excessive amounts of time on the Internet, playing games, engaging in online "chat groups," printing multiple copies of documents, or otherwise creating unnecessary network traffic.

SAMPLE CLAUSES

Allowed use of computer system. The computer system is the property of XYZ Corporation and may be used only for legitimate business purposes. Users are permitted access to the computer system to assist them in the performance of their jobs. All users have the responsibility to use computer resources professionally, ethically, and lawfully. Use of the computer system is a privilege that may be revoked at any time.

[*This clause limits use of the computer system to legitimate business purposes only and does not allow for any personal use.*]

Allowed use of computer system (alternative language).
The computer system is the property of XYZ Corporation
and may only be used for approved purposes. Users are permitted access to the computer system to assist them in the
performance of their jobs. Occasional, limited, appropriate personal use of the computer system is permitted if the use does
not (1) interfere with the user's work performance; (2) interfere with any other user's work performance; (3) have undue
impact on the operation of the computer system; or (4) violate
any other provision of this policy or any other policy, guideline,
or standard of XYZ Corporation. At all times, users have the
responsibility to use computer resources in a professional, ethical, and lawful manner. Personal use of the computer system is
a privilege that may be revoked at any time.

[*This clause recognizes that certain personal uses are allowed, but
that the uses must not interfere with the operation of the business.
This type of clause should be considered carefully. Allowing any personal use of the computer system may prevent the company from
discriminating against certain message content (for example,
union-organizing activities).*]

Prohibited uses. Without prior written permission from
_____, XYZ Corporation's computer system may not
be used for dissemination or storage of commercial or personal advertisements, solicitations, promotions, destructive programs (that is, viruses or self-replicating code), political material,
or any other unauthorized use.

[*It is sometimes helpful to specifically identify the types of use that
is prohibited.*]

Duty not to waste computer resources. Users must not
deliberately perform acts that waste computer resources or
unfairly monopolize resources to the exclusion of others. These
acts include, but are not limited to, sending mass mailings or
chain letters, subscribing to nonbusiness-related listservers and
mailing lists, spending excessive amounts of time on the
Internet, playing games, engaging in online "chat groups," printing multiple copies of documents, or otherwise creating unnec-

essary network traffic. Because audio, video, and picture files require significant storage space, these files of this sort may not be downloaded unless they are business-related.

[*Computer resources are not unlimited. There is finite bandwidth on the network and limited storage capacity. Employees should be aware of their duty to conserve these valuable resources.*]

Expectations of Privacy

The policy should explicitly define what privacy rights, if any, employees have in the material they create or receive on the computer. In most instances, the policy contains an express waiver of privacy rights and specifically states that employees should have no expectation of privacy in anything they create, store, send, or receive on the computer system.

Monitoring

If the employer intends to monitor employee computer use, monitoring should be specifically addressed in the policy. Employees should understand that their messages and files may be reviewed at any time, without prior notice. In general, employers refer to monitoring as a "right" but not a duty. Employers want the right to review files and messages on their system when necessary, but not to obligate themselves to read every message. Employers do not want a situation to arise where employees believe their employer has assumed a duty to protect them from any and all inappropriate or offensive e-mail. In such an instance, a sensitive employee might sue the employer for negligence if it fails to detect and stop a message with an off-color joke from reaching the employee.

Care in Drafting E-mail

Employees must understand the unique nature of e-mail. It cannot easily be deleted. It can be copied and forwarded with ease. It is a growing focus of litigation. The quality of employees' writing, even in e-mail, reflects on the business. This last element, care in drafting, is critical to minimizing your business's potential liability. If employees treat e-mail like any other formal business communication, many potential claims for discrimination, harassment, and defamation are likely to be avoided.

SAMPLE CLAUSE

User's duty of care. Users should endeavor to make each electronic communications truthful and accurate. Users should use the same care in drafting e-mail and other electronic documents as they would for any other written communication. The quality of writing reflects on the company. Users should always strive to use good grammar and correct punctuation, and keep in mind that anything created or stored on the computer system may, and likely will, be reviewed by others.
[*The primary cause of litigation involving e-mail is that it is treated far too informally. This clause urges employees to use care in drafting their messages.*]

Avoid Inappropriate Content

Spelling out the specific types of content that should be avoided in e-mail may seem simplistic and unnecessary. But it is important to make sure employees understand that certain types of messages simply cannot and will not be tolerated.

SAMPLE CLAUSE

Prohibited activities. Material that is fraudulent, harassing, embarrassing, sexually explicit, profane, obscene, intimidating, defamatory, or otherwise unlawful or inappropriate may not be sent by e-mail or other form of electronic communication (such as bulletin board systems, newsgroups, chat groups) or displayed on or stored in XYZ Corporation's computers. Users encountering or receiving this kind of material should immediately report the incident to their supervisor.

[*This is an example of a catch-all clause defining inappropriate content for e-mail. This clause can be expanded or refined to address particular areas of concern. For example, language could be included to address off-color or discriminatory jokes or cartoons.*]

Employee Sign-off

To ensure that employees take the computer and e-mail use policy seriously, they should be required to sign and date the policy and acknowledge that they understand that violations may result in disciplinary action, including possible termination. In the event of a later dispute, a signed policy serves as evidence that the particular employee read the policy and that the employer took affirmative steps to police its system. For example, if an employee sued his employer for invasion of privacy for monitoring e-mail, the employer could introduce the policy into evidence at trial to show that it had the employee's consent to monitor. The policy could also serve as evidence in a harassment case to show an employer's overall efforts to combat inappropriate conduct in the workplace.

SAMPLE CLAUSE

Acknowledgment. Here is a an example of a clause confirming the employee's acknowledgment of the policy:

> I have read and agree to comply with the terms of this policy governing use of XYZ Corporation's computer network. I understand that a violation of this policy may result in disciplinary action, including possible termination, as well as civil and criminal liability.
>
> Date _____   _____
>   Signature
>
>   _____
>   Printed name

Before adopting a policy, an employer should consider how binding the policy will be. Some courts have held that an employer may be contractually bound by the terms set forth in employee manuals and policies. To avoid potential disputes as to the binding nature of the policy, the policy should make clear that it does not grant the employee any contractual rights.

Summary

Although the computer and e-mail use policy you design for your business may have dozens of clauses, it is important to focus on a handful of underlying principles. By emphasizing these principles, you take a significant step toward minimizing potential liability.

Chapter 13

Ensuring Employee Compliance With Policies

Education, Education, Education . . .

For best results, constructing an e-mail policy should be a cooperative process. The human relations department generally spearheads the project, with input from members of the information systems department, senior management, corporate counsel, and even employees and their unions. Although it may not be possible to develop a consensus for every provision in the proposed policy (making it necessary for management to impose certain terms), open discussion promotes appreciation for employee expectations and concerns and eases implementation of the policy once it is completed.

Preparing and adopting a computer and e-mail use policy is only half the battle. The principles, duties, and obligations set forth in the policy must be the subject of continuing efforts to educate employees. Merely having employees sign the policy and placing a copy in their files is not enough. The policy should be periodically recirculated[1] to employees and regularly revised to reflect changes in the law.

Some businesses have employees `sign their computer and e-mail use policies again every quarter. Other businesses have their policies automatically appear online periodically as part of the logon process to their computer networks. Employees must specifically click on an "I agree and accept" button to complete the logon process. This method is known as a "click-wrap agreement." Another approach is to have the employee actually type *I accept*. The latter approach may provide even stronger evidence of the employee's acceptance of the terms of the policy.

In addition to reviewing the policy periodically with employees, most businesses should also consider sponsoring consciousness-raising seminars or training sessions for their employees to specifically address proper use of the computer and e-mail systems.

Sending regular "reminder memos" to employees is another technique used by businesses to ensure that the principles set forth in their computer and e-mail use policies are fulfilled. These memos are typically only a paragraph or two in length and focus on a single topic. Suggested topics include: proper e-mail security, e-mail etiquette, proper use of copyrighted material, and inappropriate e-mail content. Illustrative memos are included in the example policies of Appendix A.

Summary

Although e-mail has been around for a relatively short time, bad habits concerning its use are already ingrained. Employees must be reeducated-through written policies, training sessions, and regular memos-to ensure that your business's computer resources are used properly and professionally. A unified approach to controlling e-mail abuse is your best protection against potential liability.

Appendix A

Example Policies

Long-Form E-mail Computer Use Policy

Computer Use Policy

Purpose

XYZ Corporation relies on its computer network to conduct its business. To ensure that its computer resources are used properly by its employees, independent contractors, agents, and other computer users, XYZ Corporation has created this Computer Use Policy (the "Policy").

The rules and obligations described in this Policy apply to all users (the "Users") of XYZ Corporation's computer network, wherever they may be located. Violations will be taken very seriously and may result in disciplinary action, including possible termination, and civil and criminal liability.

It is every employee's duty to use XYZ Corporation's computer resources responsibly, professionally, ethically, and lawfully.

Definitions

From time to time in this Policy, we refer to terms that require definitions:

The term *Computer Resources* refers to XYZ Corporation's entire computer network. Specifically, Computer Resources includes, but are not limited to: host computers, file servers, application servers, communication servers, mail servers, fax servers, Web servers, workstations, stand-alone computers, laptops, software, data files, and all internal and external computer and communications networks (for example, Internet, commercial online services, value-added networks, e-mail systems) that may be accessed directly or indirectly from our computer network.

The term *Users* refers to all employees, independent contractors, consultants, temporary workers, and other persons or entities who use our Computer Resources.

Policy

The Computer Resources are the property of XYZ Corporation and may be used only for legitimate business purposes. Users are permitted access to the Computer Resources to assist them in performance of their jobs. Use of the computer system is a privilege that may be revoked at any time.

In using or accessing our Computer Resources, Users must comply with the following provisions.

A. No Expectation of Privacy

No expectation of privacy. The computers and computer accounts given to Users are to assist them in performance of their jobs. Users should not have an expectation of privacy in anything they create, store, send, or receive on the computer system. The computer system belongs to the company and may be used only for business purposes.

Waiver of privacy rights. Users expressly waive any right of privacy in anything they create, store, send, or receive on the computer or through the Internet or any other computer network. Users consent to allowing personnel of the company to access and review all materials Users create, store, send, or receive on the computer or through the Internet or any other computer network. Users understand that XYZ Corporation may use human or automated means to monitor use of its Computer Resources.

B. Prohibited Activities

Inappropriate or unlawful material. Material that is fraudulent, harassing, embarrassing, sexually explicit, profane, obscene, intimidating, defamatory, or otherwise unlawful or inappropriate may not be sent by e-mail or other form of electronic communication (such as bulletin board systems, newsgroups, chat groups) or displayed on or stored in XYZ Corporation's computers. Users encountering or receiving this kind of material should immediately report the incident to their supervisors.

Prohibited uses. Without prior written permission from _____, XYZ Corporation's Computer Resources may not be used for dissemination or storage of commercial or personal advertisements, solicitations, promotions, destructive programs (that is, viruses or self-replicating code), political material, or any other unauthorized use.

Waste of computer resources. Users may not deliberately perform acts that waste Computer Resources or unfairly monopolize resources to the exclusion of others. These acts include, but are not limited to, sending mass mailings or chain letters, spending excessive amounts of time on the Internet, playing games, engaging in online chat groups, printing multiple copies of documents, or otherwise creating unnecessary network traffic.

Misuse of software. Without prior written authorization from _____, Users may not do any of the following: (1) copy software for use on their home computers; (2) provide copies of software to any independent contractors or clients of XYZ Corporation or to any third person; (3) install software on any of XYZ Corporation's workstations or servers; (4) download any software from the Internet or other online service to any of XYZ Corporation's workstations or servers; (5) modify, revise, transform, recast, or adapt any software; or (6) reverse-engineer, disassemble, or decompile any software. Users who become aware of any misuse of software or violation of copyright law should immediately report the incident to their supervisors.

Communication of trade secrets. Unless expressly authorized by _____, sending, transmitting, or otherwise disseminating proprietary data, trade secrets, or other confidential information of the company is strictly prohibited. Unauthorized dissemination of this information may result in substantial civil liability as well as severe criminal penalties under the Economic Espionage Act of 1996.

C. Passwords

Responsibility for passwords. Users are responsible for safeguarding their passwords for access to the computer system. Individual passwords should not be printed, stored online, or given to others. Users are responsible for all transactions made using their passwords. No User may access the computer system with another User's password or account.

Passwords do not imply privacy. Use of passwords to gain access to the computer system or to encode particular files or messages does not imply that Users have an expectation of privacy in the material they create or receive on the computer system. XYZ Corporation has global passwords that permit it access to all material stored on its computer system-regardless of whether that material has been encoded with a particular User's password.

D. Security

Accessing other user's files. Users may not alter or copy a file belonging to another User without first obtaining permission from the owner of the file. Ability to read, alter, or copy a file belonging to another User does not imply permission to read, alter, or copy that file. Users may not use the computer system to "snoop" or pry into the affairs of other users by unnecessarily reviewing their files and e-mail.

Accessing other computers and networks. A User's ability to connect to other computer systems through the network or by a modem does not imply a right to connect to those systems or to make use of those systems unless specifically authorized by the operators of those systems.

Computer security. Each User is responsible for ensuring that use of outside computers and networks, such as the Internet, does not compromise the security of XYZ Corporation's Computer Resources. This duty includes taking reasonable precautions to prevent intruders from accessing the company's network without authorization and to prevent introduction and spread of viruses.

E. VIRUSES

Virus detection. Viruses can cause substantial damage to computer systems. Each User is responsible for taking reasonable precautions to ensure he or she does not introduce viruses into XYZ Corporation's network. To that end, all material received on floppy disk or other magnetic or optical medium and all material downloaded from the Internet or from computers or networks that do not belong to XYZ Corporation MUST be scanned for viruses and other destructive programs before being placed onto the computer system. Users should understand that their home computers and laptops may contain viruses. All disks transferred from these computers to XYZ Corporation's network MUST be scanned for viruses.

Accessing the Internet. To ensure security and avoid the spread of viruses, Users accessing the Internet through a computer attached to XYZ Corporation's network must do so through an approved Internet firewall. Accessing the Internet directly, by modem, is strictly prohibited unless the computer you are using is not connected to the company's network.

F. ENCRYPTION SOFTWARE

Use of encryption software. Users may not install or use encryption software on any of XYZ Corporation's computers without first obtaining written permission from their supervisors. Users may not use passwords or encryption keys that are unknown to their supervisors.

Export restrictions. The federal government has imposed restrictions on export of programs or files containing encryption technology (such as e-mail programs that permit encryption of messages and electronic commerce software that encodes transactions). Software containing encryption technology is not to be placed on the Internet or transmitted in any way outside the United States without prior written authorization from _____.

G. MISCELLANEOUS

Attorney-client communications. E-mail sent from or to in-house counsel or an attorney representing the company should include this warning header on each page: "ATTORNEY-CLIENT PRIVILEGED; DO NOT FORWARD WITHOUT PERMISSION."

Compliance with applicable laws and licenses. In their use of Computer Resources, Users must comply with all software licenses; copyrights; and all other state, federal, and international laws governing intellectual property and online activities.

Other policies applicable. In their use of Computer Resources, Users must observe and comply with all other policies and guidelines of the company, including but not limited to the following:

[Note: additions, if any]

Amendments and revisions. This Policy may be amended or revised from time to time as the need arises. Users will be provided with copies of all amendments and revisions.

No additional rights. This Policy is not intended to, and does not grant, Users any contractual rights.

I have read and agree to comply with the terms of this Policy governing use of XYZ Corporation's Computer Resources. I understand that a violation of this Policy may result in disciplinary action, including possible termination, as well as civil or criminal liability.

Date _____   _____

                              Signature

                              _____

                              Printed name

Short Form E-mail and Computer Use Policy

To maximize the benefits of its computer resources and minimize potential liability, XYZ Corporation has created this policy. All computer users are obligated to use these resources responsibly, professionally, ethically, and lawfully.

You are given access to our computer network to assist you in performing your job. You should not have an expectation of privacy in anything you create, store, send, or receive on the computer system. The computer system belongs to the company and may only be used for business purposes. Without prior notice, the company may review any material created, stored, sent, or received on its network or through the Internet or any other computer network.

Use of computer resources for any of these activities is strictly prohibited:

- Sending, receiving, downloading, displaying, printing, or otherwise disseminating material that is sexually explicit, profane, obscene, harassing, fraudulent, racially offensive, defamatory, or otherwise unlawful
- Disseminating or storing commercial or personal advertisements, solicitations, promotions, destructive programs (that is, viruses or self-replicating code), political information, or any other unauthorized material
- Wasting computer resources by, among other things, sending mass mailings or chain letters, spending excessive amounts of time on the Internet, playing games, engaging in online chat groups, printing multiple copies of documents, or otherwise creating unnecessary network traffic
- Using or copying software in violation of a license agreement or copyright
- Violating any state, federal, or international law

If you become aware of someone using computer resources for any of these activities, you are obligated to report the incident immediately to your supervisor.

Violations of this policy will be taken seriously and may result in disciplinary action, including possible termination, and civil and criminal liability.

I have read and agree to comply with terms of this policy.

Date _____   _____
                                  Signature

                                  _____
                                  Printed name

Internet Use Policy

Certain employees may be provided with access to the Internet to assist them in performing their jobs. The Internet can be a valuable source of information and research. In addition, e-mail can provide excellent means of communicating with other employees, our customers and clients, outside vendors, and other businesses. Use of the Internet, however, must be tempered with common sense and good judgment.

If you abuse your right to use the Internet, it will be taken away from you. In addition, you may be subject to disciplinary action, including possible termination, and civil and criminal liability.

Your use of the Internet is governed by this policy.

Disclaimer of liability for use of Internet. XYZ Corporation is not responsible for material viewed or downloaded by users from the Internet. The Internet is a worldwide network of computers that contains millions of pages of information. Users are cautioned that many of these pages include offensive, sexually explicit, and inappropriate material. In general, it is difficult to avoid at least some contact with this material while using the Internet. Even innocuous search requests may lead to sites with highly offensive content. In addition, having an e-mail address on the Internet may lead to receipt of unsolicited e-mail containing offensive content. Users accessing the Internet do so at their own risk.

Employee's duty of care. Employees should endeavor to make each electronic communication truthful and accurate. You should use the same care in drafting e-mail and other electronic documents as you would for any other written communication. Please keep in mind that anything created or stored on the computer system may, and likely will, be reviewed by others.

Duty not to waste computer resources. Employees must not deliberately perform acts that waste computer resources or unfairly monopolize resources to the exclusion of others. These acts include, but are not limited to, sending mass mailings or chain letters, spending excessive amounts of time on the Internet, playing games, engaging in online chat groups, printing multiple copies of documents, or otherwise creating unnecessary network traffic. Because audio, video, and picture files require significant storage space, files of this sort may not be downloaded unless they are business-related.

No expectation of privacy. The computers and computer accounts given to employees are to assist them in performance of their jobs. Employees should not have an expectation of privacy in anything they create, store, send, or receive on the computer system. The computer system belongs to the company and may only be used for business purposes.

No privacy in communications. Employees should never consider electronic communications to be either private or secure. E-mail may be stored indefinitely on any number of computers, including that of the recipient. Copies of your messages may be forwarded to others either electronically or on paper. In addition, e-mail sent to nonexistent or incorrect usernames may be delivered to persons that you never intended.

Monitoring of computer usage. The company has the right, but not the duty, to monitor any and all aspects of its computer system, including, but not limited to, monitoring sites visited by employees on the Internet, monitoring chat groups and newsgroups, reviewing material downloaded or uploaded by users to the Internet, and reviewing e-mail sent and received by users.

Blocking of inappropriate content. The company may use software to identify inappropriate or sexually explicit Internet sites. Such sites may be blocked from access by company networks. In the event you nonetheless encounters inappropriate or sexually explicit material while browsing on the Internet, immediately disconnect from the site, regardless of whether the site was subject to company blocking software.

Prohibited activities. Material that is fraudulent, harassing, embarrassing, sexually explicit, profane, obscene, intimidating, defamatory, or otherwise unlawful or inappropriate may not be sent by e-mail or other form of electronic communication (bulletin board systems, newsgroups, chat groups), downloaded from the Internet, or displayed on or stored in XYZ

Corporation's computers. Employees encountering or receiving this kind of material should immediately report the incident to their supervisors.

Games and entertainment software. Employees may not use the company's Internet connection to download games or other entertainment software, including screen savers, or to play games over the Internet.

Illegal copying. Employees may not illegally copy material protected under copyright law or make that material available to others for copying. You are responsible for complying with copyright law and applicable licenses that may apply to software, files, graphics, documents, messages, and other material you wish to download or copy. You may not agree to a license or download any material for which a registration fee is charged without first obtaining the express written permission of _____.

Accessing the Internet. To ensure security and avoid the spread of viruses, employees accessing the Internet through a computer attached to XYZ Corporation's network must do so through an approved Internet firewall. Accessing the Internet directly, by modem, is strictly prohibited unless the computer you are using is not connected to the company's network.

Virus detection. Files obtained from sources outside the company, including disks brought from home; files downloaded from the Internet, newsgroups, bulletin boards, or other online services; files attached to e-mail; and files provided by customers or vendors, may contain dangerous computer viruses that may damage the company's computer network. Employees should never download files from the Internet, accept e-mail attachments from outsiders, or use disks from noncompany sources, without first scanning the material with company-approved virus checking software. If you suspect that a virus has been introduced into the company's network, notify _____ immediately.

Sending unsolicited e-mail (spamming). Without the express permission of their supervisors, employees may not send unsolicited e-mail to persons with whom they do not have a prior relationship.

Altering attribution information. Employees must not alter the "From:" line or other attribution-of-origin information in e-mail, messages, or postings. Anonymous or pseudonymous electronic communications are forbidden. Employees must identify themselves honestly and accurately when participating in chat groups, making postings to newsgroups, sending e-mail, or otherwise communicating online.

Standard footers for e-mail. This footer should be appended to all e-mail sent outside the company:

This e-mail and any files transmitted with it are confidential and are intended solely for the use of the individual or entity to whom they are addressed. This communication may contain material protected by the attorney-client privilege. If you are not the intended recipient or the person responsible for delivering the e-mail to the intended recipient, be advised that you have received this e-mail in error and that any use, dissemination, forwarding, printing, or copying of this e-mail is strictly prohibited. If you have received this e-mail in error, please immediately notify _____ by telephone at _____. You will be reimbursed for reasonable costs incurred in notifying us.

Attorney-client communications. E-mail sent from or to in-house counsel or an attorney representing the company should include this warning header on each page: "ATTORNEY-CLIENT PRIVILEGED; DO NOT FORWARD WITHOUT PERMISSION." Communications from attorneys may not be forwarded without the sender's express permission.

Use of encryption software. Employees may not install or use encryption software on any of XYZ Corporation's computers without first obtaining written permission from their supervisors. You must not use passwords or encryption keys that are unknown to your supervisor.

Export restrictions. The federal government has imposed restrictions on export of programs or files containing encryption technology (such as e-mail programs that permit encryption of messages and electronic commerce software that encodes transactions). Software containing encryption technology is not to be placed on the Internet or transmitted in any way outside the United States without prior written authorization from _____.

Other policies applicable. In their use of the Internet, users must observe and comply with all other policies and guidelines of the company, including but not limited to the following:

[Note: additions, if any]

Amendments and revisions. This policy may be amended or revised from time to time as the need arises. Users will be provided with copies of all amendments and revisions.

Violations of this policy will be taken seriously and may result in disciplinary action, including possible termination, and civil and criminal liability.

I have read and agree to comply with the terms of this policy.

Date _____   _____

                                     Signature

                                _____

                                     Printed name

Guidelines for Employee Use of E-mail

E-mail is quickly becoming one of our most important methods of communicating with each other and with our clients, customers, vendors, and consultants. To maximize the benefits of this new medium and minimize potential liability, XYZ Corporation has created the following guidelines. Please keep in mind that these guidelines are not intended to discourage your use of e-mail in performing your job. Rather, they are intended to ensure that e-mail is used responsibly and with discretion.

You should never consider your electronic communications to be either private or secure. E-mail may be stored indefinitely on any number of computers, including that of the recipient. Copies of your messages may be forwarded to others either electronically or on paper. In addition, e-mail sent to nonexistent or incorrect usernames may be delivered to persons that you never intended.

In using the e-mail system, you must comply with the following guidelines.

THINK before sending a message. It is very important that you use the same care and discretion in drafting e-mail as you would for any other written communication. Anything created or stored on the computer may, and likely will, be reviewed by others. Before sending a message, ask yourself the following question: Would I want a judge or jury to see this message?

Inappropriate material. Material that is fraudulent, harassing, embarrassing, sexually explicit, profane, obscene, intimidating, defamatory, or otherwise unlawful or inappropriate may not be sent by e-mail. If you encounter this kind of material, you are obliged to report it to your supervisor.

Do not forward or initiate chain e-mail. Chain e-mail is a message sent to a number of people asking each recipient to send copies with the same message to a specified number of others. Do not forward e-mail to any person or entity without the express permission of the sender.

Alterations. Never alter the "From:" line or other attribu-tion-of-origin information on your e-mail. Anonymous or pseu-donymous messages are forbidden.

Employees who fail to comply with these guidelines may be subject to disciplinary action, including revocation of e-mail privileges. Repeated violations of this policy may result in termination.

Chain or Mass E-mail Memo

This is a reminder that XYZ Corporation provides its computer system and access to e-mail for legitimate business purposes only. Every employee is expected to use good judgment when using the e-mail system. Sending chain e-mail or nonbusiness-related mass e-mail violates this standard and will not be tolerated.

Chain e-mail is a message sent to a number of people asking each recipient to send copies with the same request to a specified number of others. *Mass e-mail* is a message sent to a large number of recipients (for example, all employees) without any legitimate business purpose. Sending either type of messages wastes our computer resources and delays delivery of essential e-mail. Circulating chain e-mail, in particular, can result in an enormous volume of messages on the network. The number of messages increases geometrically if the instructions are followed by all recipients. This can seriously degrade network performance and consume substantial amounts of valuable disk space and computer memory.

Employees should delete all chain e-mail and all nonbusiness-related mass e-mail immediately upon receipt and refrain from forwarding them to any other employees. Any employee receiving a chain e-mail or a nonbusiness-related mass e-mail should report the incident to _____.

Employees found to be involved in sending chain e-mail or nonbusiness-related mass e-mail may be subject to disciplinary action, including revocation of e-mail privileges. Repeated violations of this policy may result in termination.

Software Policy Statement

Purpose

This policy is adopted to ensure proper use of software owned by and licensed to XYZ Corporation. The following policy, rules, and conditions apply to all users of XYZ Corporation's computer resources and services, wherever they are located. Violations of this policy may result in disciplinary action, including possible termination, or legal action.

Policy

Software may only be used in compliance with the terms of the applicable license agreements.

Without prior written authorization from the software manager, employees may not do any of the following:

- Copy software for use on their home computers
- Provide copies of software to any independent contractors or clients of XYZ Corporation or to any third person
- Install software on any of XYZ Corporation's workstations or servers
- Download any software from the Internet or other online service to any of XYZ Corporation's workstations or servers
- Modify, revise, transform, recast, or adapt any software
- Reverse-engineer, disassemble, or decompile any software

Employees who become aware of any misuse of software or violation of this policy should report the incident to the software manager immediately.

This policy may be amended from time to time as the need arises.

I have read and agree to comply with the foregoing policy, rules, and conditions governing use of XYZ Corporation's software and computer resources. I understand that a violation of this policy may result in disciplinary action, including possible termination, or legal action.

Date _____   _____

                                          Signature

                                          _____

                                          Printed name[1]

Endnote

1. Copyright © 1997 by Network World Inc., 161 Worcester Road, Framingham, MA 01701. This policy originally appeared in connection with an article the author wrote on software audits. The article, entitled "Surviving an Audit," appeared in the Nov. 17, 1997, issue of *Network World* magazine. The policy is reprinted here with permission.

Appendix B

Selected Laws and Regulations

Electronic Communications Privacy Act

§ 2511. Interception and disclosure of wire, oral, or electronic communications prohibited

(1) Except as otherwise specifically provided in this chapter [18 USCS §§2510 et seq.] any person who—

(a) intentionally intercepts, endeavors to intercept, or procures any other person to intercept or endeavor to intercept, any wire, oral, or electronic communication;

(b) intentionally uses, endeavors to use, or procures any other person to use or endeavor to use any electronic, mechanical, or other device to intercept any oral communication when—

(i) such device is affixed to, or otherwise transmits a signal through, a wire, cable, or other like connection used in wire communication; or

(ii) such device transmits communications by radio, or interferes with the transmission of such communication; or

(iii) such person knows, or has reason to know, that such device or any component thereof has been sent through the mail or transported in interstate or foreign commerce; or

(iv) such use or endeavor to use (A) takes place on the premises of any business or other commercial establishment the operations of which affect interstate or foreign commerce; or (B) obtains or is for the purpose of obtaining information relating to the operations of any business or other commercial establishment the operations of which affect interstate or foreign commerce; or

(v) such person acts in the District of Columbia, the Commonwealth of Puerto Rico, or any territory or possession of the United States;

(c) intentionally discloses, or endeavors to disclose, to any other person the contents of any wire, oral, or electronic communication, knowing or having reason to know that the information was obtained through the interception of a wire, oral, or electronic communication in violation of this subsection;

(d) intentionally uses, or endeavors to use, the contents of any wire, oral, or electronic communication, knowing or having reason to know that the information was obtained through the interception of a wire, oral, or electronic communication in violation of this subsection; or

(e)

(i) intentionally discloses, or endeavors to disclose, to any other person the contents of any wire, oral, or electronic communication, intercepted by means authorized by sections 2511(2)(A)(ii), 2511(b)-(c),b 2511(e), 2516, and 2518 of this subchapter [chapter],

(ii) knowing or having reason to know that the information was obtained through the interception of such a communication in connection with a criminal investigation,

(iii) having obtained or received the information in connection with a criminal investigation, and

(iv) with intent to improperly obstruct, impede, or interfere with a duly authorized criminal investigation,

shall be punished as provided in subsection (4) or shall be subject to suit as provided in subsection (5).

(2)(a)(i) It shall not be unlawful under this chapter [18 USCS §§2510 et seq.] for an operator of a switchboard, or an officer, employee, or agent of a provider of wire or electronic communication service, whose facilities are used in the transmission of a wire or electronic communication, to intercept, disclose, or use that communication in the normal course of his employment while engaged in any activity which is a necessary incident to the rendition of his service or to the protection of the rights or property of the provider of that service, except that a provider of wire communication service to the public shall not utilize service observing or random monitoring except for mechanical or service quality control checks.

(ii) Notwithstanding any other law, providers of wire or electronic communication service, their officers, employees, and agents, landlords, custodians, or other persons, are authorized to provide information, facilities, or technical assistance to persons authorized by law to intercept wire, oral, or electronic communications or to conduct electronic surveillance, as defined in section 101 of the Foreign Intelligence Surveillance Act of 1978 [50 USCS §1801] if such provider, its officers, employees, or agents, landlord, custodian, or other specified person, has been provided with—

(A) a court order directing such assistance signed by the authorizing judge, or

(B) a certification in writing by a person specified in section 2518(7) of this title or the Attorney General of the United States that no warrant or court order is required by law, that all statutory requirements have been met, and that the specified assistance is required, setting forth the period of time during which the provision of the information, facilities, or technical assistance is authorized and specifying the information, facilities, or technical assistance required. No provider of wire or electronic communication service, officer, employee, or agent thereof, or landlord, custodian, or other specified person shall disclose the existence of any interception or surveillance or the device used to accomplish the interception or surveillance with respect to which the person has been furnished an order or certification under this subparagraph, except as may otherwise be required by legal process and then only after prior notification to the Attorney General or to the principal prosecuting attorney of a State or any political subdivision of a State, as may be appropriate. Any such disclosure, shall render such person liable for the civil damages provided for in section 2520. No cause of action shall lie in any court against any provider of wire or electronic communication service, its officers, employees, or agents, landlord, custodian, or other specified person for providing information, facilities, or assistance in accordance with the terms of a court order or certification under this chapter [18 USCS §§2510 et seq.].

(b) It shall not be unlawful under this chapter [18 USCS §§2510 et seq.] for an officer, employee, or agent of the Federal Communications Commission, in the normal course of his employment and in discharge of the monitoring responsibilities exercised by the Commission in the enforcement of chapter 5 of title 47 [47 USCS §§151 et seq.] of the United States Code, to intercept a wire or electronic communication, or oral communication transmitted by radio, or to disclose or use the information thereby obtained.

(c) It shall not be unlawful under this chapter [18 USCS §§2510 et seq.] for a person acting under color of law to intercept a wire, oral, or electronic communication, where such person is a party to the communication or one of the parties to the communication has given prior consent to such interception.

(d) It shall not be unlawful under this chapter [18 USCS §§2510 et seq.] for a person not acting under color of law to intercept a wire, oral, or electronic communication where such person is a party to the communication or where one of the parties to the communication has given prior consent to such interception unless such communication is intercepted for the purpose of committing any criminal or tortious act in violation of the Constitution or laws of the United States or of any State.

(e) Notwithstanding any other provision of this title or section 705 or 706 of the Communications Act of 1934 [47 USCS §605 or 606], it shall not be unlawful for an officer, employee, or agent of the United States in the normal course of his official duty to conduct electronic surveillance, as defined in section 101 of the Foreign Intelligence Surveillance Act of 1978 [50 USCS §1801], as authorized by that Act [50 USCS §§1801 et seq.].

(f) Nothing contained in this chapter [18 USCS §§2510 et seq.] or chapter 121 [18 USCS §§2701 et seq.], or section 705 of the Communications Act of 1934 [47 USCS §605], shall be deemed to affect the acquisition by the United States Government of foreign intelligence information from international or foreign communications, or foreign intelligence activities conducted in accordance with otherwise applicable Federal law involving a foreign electronic communications system, utilizing a means other than electronic surveillance as defined in section 101 of the Foreign Intelligence Surveillance Act of 1978 [50 USCS §1801], and procedures in this chapter [18 USCS §§2510 et seq.] and the Foreign Intelligence Surveillance Act of 1978 [50 USCS §§1801 et seq.] shall be the exclusive means by which electronic surveillance, as defined in section 101 of such Act [50 USCS §1801], and the interception of domestic wire, oral, or electronic communications may be conducted.

(g) It shall not be unlawful under this chapter [18 USCS §§2510 et seq.] or chapter 121 of this title [18 USCS §§2701 et seq.] for any person—

(i) to intercept or access an electronic communication made through an electronic communication system that is configured so that such electronic communication is readily accessible to the general public;

(ii) to intercept any radio communication which is transmitted—

(I) by any station for the use of the general public, or that relates to ships, aircraft, vehicles, or persons in distress;

(II) by any governmental, law enforcement, civil defense, private land mobile, or public safety communications system, including police and fire, readily accessible to the general public;

(III) by a station operating on an authorized frequency within the bands allocated to the amateur, citizens band, or general mobile radio services; or

(IV) by any marine or aeronautical communications system;

(iii) to engage in any conduct which—

(I) is prohibited by section 633 of the Communications Act of 1934 [47 USCS §553]; or

(II) is excepted from the application of section 705(a) of the Communications Act of 1934 [47 USCS §605(a)] by section 705(b) of that Act [47 USCS §605(b)];

(iv) to intercept any wire or electronic communication the transmission of which is causing harmful interference to any lawfully operating station or consumer electronic equipment, to the extent necessary to identify the source of such interference; or

(v) for other users of the same frequency to intercept any radio communication made through a system that utilizes frequencies monitored by individuals engaged in the provision or the use of such system, if such communication is not scrambled or encrypted.

(h) It shall not be unlawful under this chapter [18 USCS §§2510 et seq.]—

(i) to use a pen register or a trap and trace device (as those terms are defined for the purposes of chapter 206 (relating to pen registers and trap and trace devices) of this title) [18 USCS §§3121 et seq.]; or

(ii) for a provider of electronic communication service to record the fact that a wire or electronic communication was initiated or completed in order to protect such provider, another provider furnishing service toward the completion of the wire or electronic communication, or a user of that service, from fraudulent, unlawful, or abusive use of such service.

(3)(a) Except as provided in paragraph (b) of this subjection, a person or entity providing an electronic communication service to the public shall not intentionally divulge the contents of any communication (other than one to such person or entity, or an agent thereof) while in transmission on that service to any person or entity other than an addressee or intended recipient of such communication or an agent of such addressee or intended recipient.

(b) A person or entity providing electronic communication service to the public may divulge the contents of any such communication—

(i) as otherwise authorized in section 2511(2)(a) or 2517 of this title;

(ii) with the lawful consent of the originator or any addressee or intended recipient of such communication;

(iii) to a person employed or authorized, or whose facilities are used, to forward such communication to its destination; or

(iv) which were inadvertently obtained by the service provider and which appear to pertain to the commission of a crime, if such divulgence is made to a law enforcement agency.

(4)(a) Except as provided in paragraph (b) of this subsection or in subsection (5), whoever violates subsection (1) of this section shall be fined under this title or imprisoned not more than five years, or both.

(b) If the offense is a first offense under paragraph (a) of this subsection and is not for a tortious or illegal purpose or for purposes of direct or indirect commercial advantage or private commercial gain, and the wire or electronic communication with respect to which the offense under paragraph (a) is a radio communication that is not scrambled , encrypted, or transmitted using modulation techniques the essential parameters of which have been withheld from the public with the intention of preserving the privacy of such communication, then—

(i) if the communication is not the radio portion of a cellular telephone communication, a cordless telephone communication that is transmitted between the cordless telephone handset and the base unit, a public land mobile radio service communication or a paging service communication, and the conduct is not that described in subsection (5), the offender shall be fined under this title or imprisoned not more than one year, or both; and

(ii) if the communication is the radio portion of a cellular telephone communication, a cordless telephone communication that is transmitted between the cordless telephone handset and the base unit, a public land mobile radio service communication or a paging service communication, the offender shall be fined under this title.

(c) Conduct otherwise an offense under this subsection that consists of or relates to the interception of a satellite transmission that is not encrypted or scrambled and that is transmitted—

(i) to a broadcasting station for purposes of retransmission to the general public; or

(ii) as an audio subcarrier intended for redistribution to facilities open to the public, but not including data transmissions or telephone calls, is not an offense under this subsection unless the conduct is for the purposes of direct or indirect commercial advantage or private financial gain.

5)(a)(i) If the communication is—

(A) a private satellite video communication that is not scrambled or encrypted and the conduct in violation of this chapter [18 USCS §§2510 et seq.] is the private viewing of that communication and is not for a tortious or illegal purpose or for purposes of direct or indirect commercial advantage or private commercial gain; or

(B) a radio communication that is transmitted on frequencies allocated under subpart D of part 74 of the rules of the Federal Communications Commission that is not scrambled or encrypted and the conduct in violation of this chapter [18 USCS §§2510 et seq.] is not for a tortious or illegal purpose or for purposes of direct or indirect commercial advantage or private commercial gain, then the person who engages in such conduct shall be subject to suit by the Federal Government in a court of competent jurisdiction.

(ii) In an action under this subsection—

(A) if the violation of this chapter [18 USCS §§2510 et seq.] is a first offense for the person under paragraph (a) of subsection (4) and such person has not been found liable in a civil action under section 2520 of this title, the Federal Government shall be entitled to appropriate injunctive relief; and

(B) if the violation of this chapter [18 USCS §§2510 et seq.] is a second or subsequent offense under paragraph (a) of subsection (4) or such person has been found liable in any prior civil action under section 2520, the person shall be subject to a mandatory $500 civil fine.

(b) The court may use any means within its authority to enforce an injunction issued under paragraph (ii) (A), and shall impose a civil fine of not less than $500 for each violation of such an injunction.

§ 2701. Unlawful access to stored communications

(a) Offense.

Except as provided in subsection (c) of this section whoever—

(1) intentionally accesses without authorization a facility through which an electronic communication service is provided; or

(2) intentionally exceeds an authorization to access that facility; and thereby obtains, alters, or prevents authorized access to a wire or electronic communication while it is in electronic storage in such system shall be punished as provided in subsection (b) of this section.

(b) Punishment.

The punishment for an offense under subsection (a) of this section is—

(1) if the offense is committed for purposes of commercial advantage, malicious destruction or damage, or private commercial gain—

(A) a fine [of]d under this title or imprisonment for not more than one year, or both, in the case of a first offense under this subparagraph; and

(B) a fine under this title or imprisonment for not more than two years, or both, for any subsequent offense under this subparagraph; and

(2) a fine [of] under this title or imprisonment for not more than six months, or both, in any other case.

(c) Exceptions.

Subsection (a) of this section does not apply with respect to conduct authorized-

(1) by the person or entity providing a wire or electronic communications service;

(2) by a user of that service with respect to a communication of or intended for that user; or

(3) in section 2703, 2704, or 2518 of this title.

Communications Decency Act

§ 230. Protection for private blocking and screening of offensive material

(a) Findings.

The Congress finds the following:

(1) The rapidly developing array of Internet and other interactive computer services available to individual Americans represent an extraordinary advance in the availability of educational and informational resources to our citizens.

(2) These services offer users a great degree of control over the information that they receive, as well as the potential for even greater control in the future as technology develops.

(3) The Internet and other interactive computer services offer a forum for a true diversity of political discourse, unique opportunities for cultural development, and myriad avenues for intellectual activity.

(4) The Internet and other interactive computer services have flourished, to the benefit of all Americans, with a minimum of government regulation.

(5) Increasingly Americans are relying on interactive media for a variety of political, educational, cultural, and entertainment services.

(b) Policy.

It is the policy of the United States—

(1) to promote the continued development of the Internet and other interactive computer services and other interactive media;

(2) to preserve the vibrant and competitive free market that presently exists for the Internet and other interactive computer services, unfettered by Federal or State regulation;

(3) to encourage the development of technologies which maximize user control over what information is received by individuals, families, and schools who use the Internet and other interactive computer services;

(4) to remove disincentives for the development and utilization of blocking and filtering technologies that empower parents to restrict their children's access to objectionable or inappropriate online material; and

(5) to ensure vigorous enforcement of Federal criminal laws to deter and punish trafficking in obscenity, stalking, and harassment by means of computer.

(c) Protection for "good samaritan"e blocking and screening of offensive material.

(1) Treatment of publisher or speaker. No provider or user of an interactive computer service shall be treated as the publisher or speaker of any information provided by another information content provider.

(2) Civil liability. No provider or user of an interactive computer service shall be held liable on account of—

(A) any action voluntarily taken in good faith to restrict access to or availability of material that the provider or user considers to be obscene, lewd, lascivious, filthy, excessively violent, harassing, or otherwise objectionable, whether or not such material is constitutionally protected; or

(B) any action taken to enable or make available to information content providers or others the technical means to restrict access to material described in paragraph (1).

(d) Effect on other laws.

(1) No effect on criminal law. Nothing in this section shall be construed to impair the enforcement of section 223 of this Act [47 USCS §223], chapter 71 (relating to obscenity) or 110 (relating to sexual exploitation of children) of title 18, United States Code [18 USCS §§1460 et seq. or §§2251 et seq.], or any other Federal criminal statute.

(2) No effect on intellectual property law. Nothing in this section shall be construed to limit or expand any law pertaining to intellectual property.

(3) State law. Nothing in this section shall be construed to prevent any State from enforcing any State law that is consistent with this section. No cause of action may be brought and no liability may be imposed under any State or local law that is inconsistent with this section.

(4) No effect on communications privacy law. Nothing in this section shall be construed to limit the application of the Electronic Communications Privacy Act of 1986 or any of the amendments made by such Act, or any similar State law.

(e) Definitions.

As used in this section:

(1) Internet. The term "Internet" means the international computer network of both Federal and non-Federal interoperable packet switched data networks.

(2) Interactive computer service. The term "interactive computer service" means any information service, system, or access software provider that provides or enables computer access by multiple users to a computer server, including specifically a service or system that provides access to the Internet and such systems operated or services offered by libraries or educational institutions.

(3) Information content provider. The term "information content provider" means any person or entity that is responsible, in whole or in part, for the creation or development of information provided through the Internet or any other interactive computer service.

(4) Access software provider. The term "access software provider" means a provider of software (including client or server software), or enabling tools that do any one or more of the following:

(A) filter, screen, allow, or disallow content;

(B) pick, choose, analyze, or digest content; or

(C) transmit, receive, display, forward, cache, search, subset, organize, reorganize, or translate content.

Economic Espionage Act of 1996

§ 1831. Economic espionage.

(a) In general—Whoever, intending or knowing that the offense will benefit any foreign government, foreign instrumentality, or foreign agent, knowingly—

(1) steals, or without authorization appropriates, takes, carries away, or conceals, or by fraud, artifice, or deception obtains a trade secret;

(2) without authorization copies, duplicates, sketches, draws, photographs, downloads, uploads, alters, destroys, photocopies, replicates, transmits, delivers, sends, mails, communicates, or conveys a trade secret;

(3) receives, buys, or possesses a trade secret, knowing the same to have been stolen or appropriated, obtained, or converted without authorization;

(4) attempts to commit any offense described in any of paragraphs (1) through (3); or

(5) conspires with one or more other persons to commit any offense described in any of paragraphs (1) through (3), and one or more of such persons do any act to effect the object of the conspiracy, shall, except as provided in subsection (b), be fined not more than $500,000 or imprisoned not more than 15 years, or both.

(b) Organizations—Any organization that commits any offense described in subsection (a) shall be fined not more than $10,000,000.

§ 1832. Theft of trade secrets.

(a) Whoever, with intent to convert a trade secret, that is related to or included in a product that is produced for or placed in interstate or foreign commerce, to the economic benefit of anyone other than the owner thereof, and intending or knowing that the offense will injure any owner of that trade secret, knowingly—

(1) steals, or without authorization appropriates, takes, carries away, or conceals, or by fraud, artifice, or deception obtains such information;

(2) without authorization copies, duplicates, sketches, draws, photographs, downloads, uploads, alters, destroys, photocopies, replicates, transmits, delivers, sends, mails, communicates, or conveys such information;

(3) receives, buys, or possesses such information, knowing the same to have been stolen or appropriated, obtained, or converted without authorization;

(4) attempts to commit any offense described in paragraphs (1) through (3); or

(5) conspires with one or more other persons to commit any offense described in paragraphs (1) through (3), and one or more of such persons do any act to effect the object of the conspiracy, shall, except as provided in subsection (b), be fined under this title or imprisoned not more than 10 years, or both.

(b) Any organization that commits any offense described in subsection (a) shall be fined not more than $5,000,000.

§ 1833. Exceptions to prohibitions.

This chapter does not prohibit—

(1) any otherwise lawful activity conducted by a governmental entity of the United States, a State, or a political subdivision of a State; or

(2) the reporting of a suspected violation of law to any governmental entity of the United States, a State, or a political subdivision of a State, if such entity has lawful authority with respect to that violation.

§ 1834. Criminal forfeiture.

(a) The court, in imposing sentence on a person for a violation of this chapter, shall order, in addition to any other sentence imposed, that the person forfeit to the United States—

(1) any property constituting or derived from any proceeds the person obtained, directly or indirectly, as the result of such violation; and

(2) any of the person's or organization's property used, or intended to be used, in any manner or part, to commit or facilitate the commission of such violation, if the court in its discretion so determines, taking into consideration the nature,

scope, and proportionality of the use of the property in the offense.

(b) Property subject to forfeiture under this section, any seizure and disposition thereof, and any administrative or judicial proceeding in relation thereto, shall be governed by section 413 of the Comprehensive Drug Abuse Prevention and Control Act of 1970 (21 U.S.C. 853), except for subsections (d) and (j) of such section, which shall not apply to forfeitures under this section.

§ 1835. Orders to preserve confidentiality

In any prosecution or other proceeding under this chapter, the court shall enter such orders and take such other action as may be necessary and appropriate to preserve the confidentiality of trade secrets, consistent with the requirements of the Federal Rules of Criminal and Civil Procedure, the Federal Rules of Evidence, and all other applicable laws. An interlocutory appeal by the United States shall lie from a decision or order of a district court authorizing or directing the disclosure of any trade secret.

§ 1836. Civil proceedings to enjoin violations

(a) The Attorney General may, in a civil action, obtain appropriate injunctive relief against any violation of this section.

(b) The district courts of the United States shall have exclusive original jurisdiction of civil actions under this subsection.

§ 1837. Applicability to conduct outside the United States

This chapter also applies to conduct occurring outside the United States if:

(1) the offender is a natural person who is a citizen or permanent resident alien of the United States, or an organization organized under the laws of the United States or a State or political subdivision thereof; or

(2) an act in furtherance of the offense was committed in the United States.

§ 1838. Construction with other laws

This chapter shall not be construed to preempt or displace any other remedies, whether civil or criminal, provided by United States Federal, State, commonwealth, possession, or territory law for the misappropriation of a trade secret, or to affect the otherwise lawful disclosure of information by any Government employees under section 552 of title 5 (commonly known as the Freedom of Information Act).

§ 1839. Definitions

As used in this chapter
   (1) the term "foreign instrumentality" means any agency, bureau, ministry, component, institution, association, or any legal, commercial, or business organization, corporation, firm, or entity that is substantially owned, controlled, sponsored, commanded, managed, or dominated by a foreign government;
   (2) the term "foreign agent" means any officer, employee, proxy, servant, delegate, or representative of a foreign government;
   (3) the term "trade secret" means all forms and types of financial, business, scientific, technical, economic, or engineering information, including patterns, plans, compilations, program devices, formulas, designs, prototypes, methods, techniques, processes, procedures, programs, or codes, whether tangible or intangible, and whether or how stored, compiled, or memorialized physically, electronically, graphically, photographically, or in writing if
   (A) the owner thereof has taken reasonable measures to keep such information secret; and
   (B) the information derives independent economic value, actual or potential, from not being generally known to, and not being readily ascertainable through proper means by the public; and
   (4) the term "owner," with respect to a trade secret, means the person or entity in whom or in which rightful legal or equitable title to or license in, the trade secret is reposed.

State Spam Statutes

Nevada Senate Bill No. 13-Senator Raggio

CHAPTER 341

AN ACT relating to actions concerning persons; providing that a person who transmits certain items of electronic mail is liable to the recipient for civil damages under certain circumstances; providing that the district court may enjoin a person from transmitting certain items of electronic mail under certain circumstances; and providing other matters properly relating thereto.

[Approved July 8, 1997]

THE PEOPLE OF THE STATE OF NEVADA, REPRESENTED IN SENATE AND ASSEMBLY, DO ENACT AS FOLLOWS:

Section 1. Chapter 41 of NRS is hereby amended by adding thereto the provisions set forth as sections 2 to 8, inclusive, of this act.

Sec. 2. As used in sections 2 to 8, inclusive, of this act, unless the context otherwise requires, the words and terms defined in sections 3 to 6, inclusive, of this act have the meanings ascribed to them in those sections.

Sec. 3. "Advertisement" means material that:
   1. Advertises for commercial purposes the availability or the quality of real property, goods, or services; or
   2. Is otherwise designed or intended to solicit a person to purchase real property, goods, or services.

Sec. 4. "Electronic mail" means a message, a file or other information that is transmitted through a local, regional, or global network, regardless of whether the message, file, or other information is:
   1. Viewed;
   2. Stored for retrieval at a later time;
   3. Printed onto paper or other similar material; or

4. Filtered or screened by a computer program that is designed or intended to filter or screen items of elec tronic mail.

Sec. 5. "Network" means a network comprised ofn one or more computers that may be accessed by a modem, electronic, or optical technology or other similar means.

Sec. 6. "Recipient" means a person who receives an item of electronic mail.

Sec. 7.

1. Except as otherwise provided in section 8 of this act, if a person transmits or causes to be transmitted to a recipient an item of electronic mail that includes an advertisement, the person is liable to the recipient for civil damages unless:

   (a) The person has a preexisting business or personal relationship with the recipient;

   (b) The recipient has expressly consented to receive the item of electronic mail from the person; or

   (c) The advertisement is readily identifiable as promotional, or contains a statement providing that it is an advertisement, and clearly and conspicuously provides:

      (1) The legal name, complete street address, and electronic mail address of the person transmitting the electronic mail; and

      (2) A notice that the recipient may decline to receive additional electronic mail that includes an advertisement from the person transmitting the electronic mail and the procedures for declining such electronic mail.

2. If a person is liable to a recipient pursuant to subsec tion 1, the recipient may recover from the person:

   (a) Actual damages or damages of $10 per item of electronic mail received, whichever is greater; and

   (b) Attorney's fees and costs.

3. In addition to any other recovery that is allowed pursuant to subsection 2, the recipient may apply to the district court of the county in which the recipient resides for an order enjoining the person from trans-

mitting to the recipient any other item of electronic mail that includes an advertisement.

<u>Sec. 8</u>.

1. If a person provides users with access to a network and, as part of that service, transmits items of electronic mail on behalf of those users, the person is immune from liability for civil damages pursuant to sections 2 to 8, inclusive, of this act, unless the person transmits an item of electronic mail that includes an advertisement he prepared or caused to be prepared.

2. The provisions of sections 2 to 8, inclusive, of this act do not apply to an item of electronic mail that is obtained by a recipient voluntarily. This subsection includes, but is not limited to, an item of electronic mail that is obtained by a recipient voluntarily from an electronic bulletin board.

<u>Sec. 9</u>. This act becomes effective on July 1, 1998.

About the Author

Michael R. Overly is Special Counsel to the Information Technology Department at the law firm of Foley & Lardner in Los Angeles. He counsels clients on software licensing, copyright, electronic commerce, and Internet and multimedia law. Overly writes and speaks frequently on these subjects. Prior to becoming an attorney, he worked as a research engineer in the Space and Technology Division of TRW Inc., Redondo Beach, California. He received his MSEE and BSEE degrees from Texas A&M University, and his J.D. from Loyola Law School in Los Angeles.

If you have any comments or suggestions concerning this book, please send them to moverly@concentric.net.

Index of Sample Clauses

Index

G

Good Samaritan provision, 51

I

Internet:
excessive use of, 84-85
monitoring employee use of, 85-86
monitoring and filtering software, 86
use policy, 107-108

L

Labor organization, 31-35
and concerted activity, 32-33
by e-mail, 31
Litigation, 15
discovery in lawsuits, 15
Listservers, 83-84
See also Computer resources.

M

Macrovirus, 78
See also Computer security.
Monitoring, 26-28, 93
automated, 29
of computer usage, 29
continuous, 27
minimizing potential liability for, 27-28
random, 27
responsive, 27